Table of Conter

5

Low Carb Cookbook for Working People & Low Carb High in Fiber:

with 299 Low Carb Recipes for Weight Loss Without Hunger 3in1

Author: Liam Sandler

content

14

15

FOREWORD

This low carb recipe book is a special book, in fact the only one of its kind in the world. You are probably wondering what is so special about this book. It's not just a book that contains 299 low carb recipes. No, it's a lot more than that! Did you know that the body is under-supplied with fiber on a conventional low-carb diet? This can happen quickly, especially with a permanent low-carb diet.

The new low-carb-high-fiber diet is intended to remedy this. It provides for a 28-day diet plan in which carbohydrates are significantly reduced, but at the same time the carbohydrates and fiber that the body really needs are taken in. In this way you maintain a healthy intestinal flora, stay full longer and can even lose weight at the same time. The effect of the low carb is not restricted. On the contrary - the burning of fat in the body is also optimally supported with high fiber, and ketosis is still possible.

So that you can benefit from this new method, we are giving you 77 low carb high fiber recipes. So you get two books in one, but wait a minute! We have another gift for you that will get you to your destination even faster and easier. You will get an online video course worth € 100

One request we have about you, do you please clear that there are no pictures of the recipes in this book. We wanted to create a book that could be sold cheaply, so we did without photos. Pictures are nice to look at but not absolutely necessary. Please refrain from writing us a bad review because there are no pictures in this book. You will also notice that some recipes were written in the you or you form. That's because different chefs worked for this book. Now we wish you a successful success and a good appetite. 9

BREAKFAST RECIPES

Crunchy omelette with cheese

248.1 kcal | Protein: 22.2 grams | Fat: 17.3 grams | Carbohydrates: 0.9 grams

Preparation time: 10 minutes

Ingredients for one serving: 1 tbsp Parmesan, finely grated | 2 eggs | 2 slices of Gouda cheese | Pepper | Rubbed thyme

Preparation: Spread
the parmesan in a non-oiled pan and let it melt slightly. In the meantime, whisk the eggs together and season them with pepper and thyme. The seasoned eggs can then be slowly poured over the melted parmesan. First spread the Gouda on top and let the egg set. Gently fold the omelette up and let it steep for a minute without heat. Now

the whole thing can be served and sprinkled with fresh herbs as required.

Delicious smoked salmon in scrambled eggs

285.7 kcal | Protein: 23.2 grams | Fat: 20.5 grams | Carbohydrates: 2.1 grams

Preparation time: 8 minutes

Ingredients for one serving:
2 eggs | 2 tbsp cream | Himalayan salt | Pepper | 1/2 teaspoon dill chopped | 50 grams of smoked salmon | some zest of an untreated organic lemon

Preparation:
Whisk the eggs with the cream and season with a little salt and pepper. Process the mixture into a scrambled egg in a non-fat frying pan. First cut the salmon into strips and mix them with the scrambled eggs. Flavor this with the zest of the lemon. Now the scrambled eggs can be served. Sprinkle generously with dill before serving. Alternatively, chives, parsley or coriander can be used.

Fried poultry debreziner with delicious fried eggs

543.2 kcal | Protein: 27.8 grams | Fat: 47.1 grams | Carbohydrates: 2 grams

Preparation time: 11 minutes

Ingredients for one serving:
2 eggs | 2 tsp vegetable oil | Salt and pepper | 1 tbsp chives cut into rolls | 2 pieces of poultry Debreziner | 3 cherry tomatoes

Preparation:
First cut the tomatoes in half and fry the eggs in a tablespoon of oil to make fried eggs. Spread the cherry tomatoes on top and season with salt and pepper. Lightly score the sausages with a knife and fry them in the remaining oil for about 3 minutes. Finally, the fried eggs can be arranged, sprinkled with chives and eaten with the debrezins.

Spicy low carb with zucchini and walnut

297.4 kcal | Protein: 52.1 grams | Fat: 41 grams | Carbohydrates: 12.5 grams **Preparation time:** 23 minutes **Ingredients for 4 muffins:** 2 eggs | 4 tbsp quark | 80 grams of almond flour | 1 pinch of baking soda | 4 tbsp chopped walnuts | 1 zucchini finely grated | Himalayan salt and pepper **Preparation:** Separate the eggs and beat the egg whites with a whisk or hand mixer to form a stiff snow. First mix the egg yolks with the quark and season the whole thing sparingly with salt and pepper. Now the almond flour can be mixed with the baking soda, the chopped nuts and the finely grated zucchini and mixed with the yolk. Carefully fold in the egg whites and fill the batter into four baking tins. Finally, the muffins are baked in the oven at 180 ° Celsius and using top and bottom heat for 15 minutes.

Delicious eggs from the oven with oregano tomatoes

204.6 kcal | Protein: 13.4 grams | Fat: 15.8 grams | Carbohydrates: 2.2 grams

Preparation time: 9 minutes

Ingredients: 2 eggs | 1 tomato | Fresh or dried oregano | Himalayan salt and pepper | 1/2 teaspoon olive oil

Preparation:
Cut the tomato into slices and layer them in a small baking dish. Now season the slices with salt, pepper and oregano and drizzle with the

olive oil. Beat the eggs over it and put the baking dish in an oven preheated to 200 ° Celsius. Now bake the eggs for 6 minutes on top and bottom heat and sprinkle with fresh herbs as required.

Fruity low carb lime quark

172.8 kcal | Protein: 17.5 grams | Fat: 6 grams | Carbohydrates: 12.2 grams

Preparation time: 6 minutes

Ingredients: 150 grams of quark | 2 tbsp cream | Juice and zest of half an untreated organic lime | 1 splash of sweetener or a little stevia | 20 grams of blackberries | 20 grams of raspberries | 20 grams of blueberries | some mint leaves or lemon balm to decorate **Preparation:** Mix the quark with the cream and flavor it with the juice and zest of the lime. First, sweeten with a sweetener if necessary. Put the whole thing in a bowl and cover everything with the berries. Before enjoying, the quark can be garnished with mint or lemon balm.

Chia pudding with strawberries

150 kcal | Protein: 8.6 grams | Fat: 6.8 grams | Carbohydrates: 13.6 grams **Preparation time:** 6 minutes - but the pudding should soak for a few hours. **Ingredients:** 150 grams of yoghurt | 1 teaspoon xylitol or stevia | 1 tsp chia seeds | some fresh thyme leaves | 80 grams of strawberries **Preparation:** Mix the yoghurt with the sweetener and the chia seeds. Now flavor with the thyme and let it soak in the refrigerator overnight. Before serving, cut the strawberries into small pieces and then fold them under. If necessary, the chia pudding can also be refined with a splash of lemon juice or a pinch of cinnamon.

Matcha yoghurt refined with mango

145 kcal | Protein: 8.9 grams | Fat: 4.6 grams | Carbohydrates: 17 grams

Preparation time: 6 minutes

Ingredients: 130 grams of yoghurt | 2 tbsp cream cheese | 1 level teaspoon matcha powder | some abrasion of an untreated organic lime | 1/2 mango

Preparation:

Mix yoghurt with cream cheese and work in the Matcha powder with a whisk. This means that there are no lumps. First, the mango can be peeled and cut into small cubes. Now lift this together with the zest of the lime under the yogurt. This yogurt can also be conveniently prepared the evening before and stored in the refrigerator.

Delicious low carb pancakes with a fruity berry sauce

343.9 kcal | Protein: 33.8 grams | Fat: 17.9 grams | Carbohydrates: 11.9 grams

Preparation time: 13 minutes

Ingredients: 2 eggs | 80 ml low-fat milk | 3 tbsp almond flour | 1 pinch of Himalayan salt | 60 grams of fresh or frozen berry mix | 1 splash of liquid sweetener | 40 ml buttermilk

Preparation:

whisk the eggs with the milk at the beginning and then stir the mixture with the almond flour. Carefully season the whole thing with a pinch of Himalayan salt. Bake small pancakes from the thick batter in a non-fat non-stick pan. Now the berries can be pureed with the buttermilk and sweetened with a sweetener. Serve the sauce with the pancakes.

Delicious grilled figs wrapped in bacon

108.6 kcal | Protein: 6.2 grams | Fat: 3 grams | Carbohydrates: 14.2 grams

Z ubereitungszeit: 6 minutes

Ingredients : 1 pear | 4 slices of raw ham such as Black Forest ham | some rosemary

Preparation:
quarter the fig, season it with finely chopped rosemary and finally wrap it in the ham. Now fry on all sides in a grill pan without fat until crispy. The figs are not only suitable for breakfast, but also as a small snack between meals.

Spicy melon salad with strips of bacon

107.2 kcal | Protein: 6.4 grams | Fat: 6 grams | Carbohydrates: 6.9

grams

Preparation time: 10 minutes

Ingredients: 120 grams of honeydew melon | Juice and zest of half an untreated organic lime | 1 tbsp lemon balm finely chopped | freshly ground black pepper | 2 tablespoons of bacon, diced

Preparation:

Cut the melon into 1 cm cubes and marinate them with the juice and zest of the lime. Mix in the lemon balm and ground pepper. Now fry the bacon in a coated pan without fat until crispy, let it cool down briefly and mix it with the melon. A slice of protein bread can be served with the melon salad. You can roast these together with the bacon in the coated pan.

Delicious pancakes made from cream cheese

337.9 kcal | Protein: 32.8 grams | Fat: 20.3 grams | Carbohydrates: 6.6 grams

Preparation time: 11 minutes

Ingredients: 50 grams of cream cheese | 2 tbsp low-fat milk | 2 eggs | 4 tbsp almond flour or coconut flour | 1 pinch of baking powder

| some vanilla flavor | 1 pinch of Himalayan salt | some sweetener, stevia or xylitol | 1 teaspoon butter

Preparation:

Mix the cream cheese with the milk. Then whisk the eggs and stir them into the mixture. First work in the almond flour and baking powder with the whisk. Now the whole thing can be seasoned with vanilla, salt and sweetener. Now the dough can be fried in a pan with melted, hot butter to make small pancakes. To get the perfect tan, sauté both sides for about 1.5 minutes.

Delicious quark with coconut and strawberry

298.8 kcal | Protein: 21.5 grams | Fat: 20.4 grams | Carbohydrates: 7.3 grams

Preparation time: 8 minutes

Ingredients: 100 grams of quark | 50 ml coconut milk | Juice of half an organic lime | some sweetener or stevia | 2 tbsp desiccated coconut, roasted | 60 grams of strawberries

Preparation:

Mix the quark with the coconut milk and then add lime juice and sweetener to taste. First, the strawberries can be cut into small pieces and stirred into the quark. Put the whole thing in a bowl and sprinkle everything with the roasted coconut flakes. This quark can also be prepared the day before and stored in the refrigerator.

Spicy low carb quark with avocado and bean sprouts

168.5 kcal | Protein: 20.4 grams | Fat: 8.1 grams | Carbohydrates: 3.5 grams

Preparation time: 8 minutes

Ingredients: 1/4 avocado | 100 grams of cottage cheese | Himalayan salt and pepper | 1 squirt of lemon juice | 10 grams of bean sprouts

Preparation:
Peel the avocado and mash it with a fork. Stir the whole thing with the quark until smooth and then season with salt, pepper and lemon juice. Now the mass can be poured into a bowl and sprinkled with the sprouts. Sprouts provide vitamins and minerals and also have almost no carbohydrates.

Energy fried eggs with delicious melted tomatoes

232.1 kcal | Protein: 13.6 grams | Fat: 18.5 grams | Carbohydrates: 2.8 grams **Preparation time:** 10 minutes **Ingredients:** 2 eggs | 1 tomato | 1 shallot | 2 teaspoons olive oil | 1/2 teaspoon rosemary finely chopped | Himalayan salt and pepper **Preparation:** Cut the tomato into six parts and remove the seeds from them. Then dice the shallot and sweat the tomato and shallot together with a teaspoon of olive oil over medium heat until translucent. First, the whole thing can be seasoned with the rosemary, salt and pepper and sautéed for 5 minutes. Fry the eggs in the remaining olive oil to make fried eggs and serve them together with the tomatoes.

Blood orange yogurt with chia seeds

111 kcal | Protein: 5.8 grams | Fat: 5 grams | Carbohydrates: 10.7 grams

Preparation time: 6 minutes The chia seeds should soak for at least 1 hour

Ingredients: 1/2 blood orange filleted | 100 grams of yogurt | 1 tsp chia seeds | some sweetener, stevia or xylitol | 1 pinch of lavender salt

Preparation:
Puree the blood orange with the yoghurt and the chia seeds in a blender. Now season the whole thing with sweetener and salt and let it soak in the fridge for about an hour.

Fruity strawberry yogurt

113.4 kcal | 8.3 grams of protein | 0.2 grams of fat | 22.6 grams of carbohydrates

Ingredients: 50gr. Strawberries | 200gr. Skimmed yoghurt

Preparation: Cut the strawberries into small pieces and then mix with the yoghurt. You can use both fresh and frozen berries. A spoonful of xylitol, xucker or sweetener is best for sweetening.

Fresh herb cottage cheese

1 47.6 kcal | 30.8 grams of protein | 0.8 grams of fat | 4.1 grams of

carbohydrates

Ingredients: 200gr. Cottage cheese (skimmed) | Herbs to your own taste

Preparation:
Mix a handful of finely chopped herbs with the cheese. You can use as many herbs as you want, depending on your taste and taste.

Classic ham and cheese scrambled eggs

338.5 kcal | 37.7 grams of protein | 20.3 grams of fat | 1.7 grams of carbohydrates **Ingredients:** 2 eggs, 50 grams of lean turkey ham , 30 grams of cheese, 1 pinch of grated Himalayan salt, 1 teaspoon of chives **Preparation:** Put the small ham cubes in a pan with a little oil and fry briefly. Then whisk the eggs and add them. Then add the cheese to the pan and finally season and sprinkle with chives.

Pancakes with fresh currants

298.2 kcal | 24 grams of protein | 17.6 grams of fat | 12.9 grams of carbohydrates **Ingredients:** 1 teaspoon coconut oil, 30 grams of currants (fresh or frozen), 2 eggs, 2 tablespoons of mineral water, 30 grams of almond flour, 1/2 teaspoon of xylitol **Preparation:** Mix the almond flour, eggs and the xylitol and slowly add the water . Coconut oil is suitable for frying the pancakes. Put this in a pan and spread evenly. Pour the batter into the pan and then add the berries. For an even browning, turn the pancakes after a short time and fry until golden.

Classic bacon and eggs

307 kcal | 22.4 grams of protein | 17.7 grams of fat | 1.2 grams of carbohydrates **Ingredients:** 2 eggs | 50 grams of breakfast bacon **Preparation:** Place the bacon on a baking rack and then bake in the oven at 200 degrees for eight minutes. Meanwhile, prepare the eggs in a pan and then serve both together.

Healthy protein bread with jam and butter

255 kcal | 12.2 grams of protein | 9.5 grams of fat | 27.7 grams of carbohydrates **Ingredients:** 2 slices of protein bread | 2 teaspoons butter and 2 teaspoons xylitol jam **Preparation:** For a nutritious and quick breakfast, brush a slice of protein bread with a little butter and then spread the jam of your choice on top.

The healthy protein bread with fresh cucumber and crunchy tomato

177.8 kcal | 11.8 grams of protein | 8.4 grams of fat | 12.2 grams of carbohydrates

Ingredients: 2 slices of protein bread | 1 tomato | ¼ cucumber **Preparation:** Cover the bread with cucumber and tomato and sprinkle the cucumber with a few squirts of lemon juice and season with chili powder. This gives your bread a special touch and that certain something.

Avocado cream with egg

236.8 kcal | 13.1 grams of protein | 17.3 grams of fat | 6.1 grams of carbohydrates **Ingredients:** 1 slice of protein bread, 1 egg, 50 grams of avocado, 1 clove of garlic, 1 pinch of Himalayan salt, 1 pinch of freshly ground pepper **Preparation:** Chop the garlic and the boiled egg. Then mash the avocado and mix with the garlic and season with salt and pepper. Then add the egg and enjoy, for example, as a delicious spread.

Low carb muesli with almond milk and oat bran

114.7 kcal | 4.2 grams of protein | 2.9 grams of fat | 16.6 grams of carbohydrates **Ingredients:** 100 ml of almond milk | 1 tbsp oat bran | 1 tbsp muesli **Preparation:** Let the oat bran swell briefly in the almond milk before you mix it with the muesli.

Apple yogurt with nuts

191.1 kcal | 5.7 grams of protein | 6.4 grams of fat | 32.1 grams of carbohydrates **Ingredients:** 1 apple, 100 grams of skimmed yoghurt, 1/2 pinch of cinnamon, 1/2 teaspoon of xylitol, 10 grams of chopped nuts, juice of an organic lime **Preparation:** Grate the apple finely and then drizzle some lime juice over it. Next, mix the apple with the yogurt and add the nuts. For a better taste, you can refine the muesli with cinnamon and xucker.

Whether for breakfast or dinner: poached eggs with crème fraîche

191.5 kcal | 13.8 grams of protein | 12.5 grams of fat | 4.1 grams of carbohydrates **Ingredients:** 2 eggs, 2 tablespoons of vinegar, 1 tablespoon of crème fraîche, 1 pinch of Himalayan salt, 1 pinch of pepper, chives for sprinkling. **Preparation** Put water in a saucepan and bring to the boil with a little vinegar. Then the water has to be cooled down to approx. 70 °. Create a strudel with the wooden spoon by stirring vigorously and then carefully slide the egg into the water. Then pull the egg white over the egg yolk with a spoon and repeat this with the second egg. Finally, brush the eggs with the crème fraîche, season with salt and pepper and sprinkle with a little chives.

The classic cheese bread in four different variations

304.5 kcal | 19.8 grams of protein | 22.3 grams of fat | 6.8 grams of carbohydrates

Ingredients: 4 slices of protein bread | 40gr. Cheese | 1 apple | Walnuts | 1 tomato | Olives

Preparation:
Brush two slices of bread with a little butter and then cut in half. Each

bread is now topped with a different cheese. Here, too, there are no limits to your imagination. Examples of healthy and tasty cheese bread would be Camembert, Gouda, Tilsiter or Gervais. To keep the bread healthy, around 40 grams of cheese are a good guideline. Now you can let off steam when topping your bread. Whether pieces of apple, tomato, cucumber, nuts or olives, these combinations are guaranteed not to make your cheese bread taste boring. Finally, season with Himalayan salt and pepper.

Aromatic curd cheese with coffee

79 kcal | 11 grams of protein | 2 grams of fat | 4 grams of carbohydrates **Ingredients:** 100 grams of quark, 1/2 teaspoon of xylitol or sweetener, 1 pinch of salt, 40 ml of espresso **Preparation:** Mix the ingredients and stir until smooth. Then put the quark in the refrigerator, because it tastes even better and fresher when it is cool!

Indian omelette

164.8 kcal | 13.8 grams of protein | 11.5 grams of fat | 1.9 grams of carbohydrates **Ingredients:** 2 eggs, 1/2 teaspoon Indian masala spice - if not available, mix curry powder with cloves, cinnamon, chilli and ginger powder, 1 tablespoon yogurt, 1 teaspoon coriander fresh or frozen **Preparation:** The eggs, den Mix the yogurt and the spices together. Don't add the coriander here yet! Then put the omelette in the pan and fry it in oil on both sides until golden. Then take out the omelette and garnish with coriander. Your exotic omelette with masala spice is ready.

Italian pepper and mozzarella breakfast

315 kcal | 19 grams of protein | 25 grams of fat | 3.5 grams of carbohydrates **Ingredients:** 1/2 bell pepper , 1 scoop of mozzarella, 2 tablespoons of olive oil, Himalayan salt and pepper as required, a few basil leaves **Preparation:** Fry the bell pepper on the skin side in a

pan. Preferably without fat. Then pull the mozzarella apart. Tip: If you pluck it apart instead of cutting it, the aroma unfolds better and ensures a great taste. Now cut the bell pepper into strips and arrange on a plate with the mozzarella. Drizzle with a little olive oil if necessary and add the basil.

Fresh fruit salad with curd cheese

183.3 kcal | 11.4 grams of protein | 0.2 grams of fat | 32.7 grams of carbohydrates **Ingredients:** 1 small banana, juice of an organic lime, 1/2 apple, 1/2 pear, 1 orange, 30 grams of pineapple, 40 grams of mixed berries, 80 grams of low-fat quark **Preparation:** Fillet the orange, slice the banana cut and then season with a little lime juice. Then cut the remaining fruit into small pieces, mix with the quark and, if necessary, sweeten with a little sweetener.

Fancy papaya-mango breakfast

61.3 kcal | 0.5 grams of protein | 0 grams of fat | 13.8 grams of carbohydrates **Ingredients:** Juice of 2 organic limes, 1/2 mango and 1/2 papaya **Preparation:** First peel the fruit and then core. Then pour some lime juice over it and let it cool in the fridge.

Delicious grilled fruits

126 kcal | 1.1 grams of protein | 0.4 grams of fat | 28.3 grams of carbohydrates **Ingredients:** 100 grams of watermelon, 1/2 papaya, 100 grams of pineapple, 1 sprig of thyme, chilli powder, Himalayan salt **Preparation:** First, the fruit is cut into approx. 1 cm thick slices. Then the fruit is fried in a pan with thyme. Now season with Himalayan salt and chilli and drizzle with lemon juice to give it that special flavor.

Refreshing melon with delicious Parma ham

303 kcal | 27.2 grams of protein | 15.2 grams of fat | 15 grams of carbohydrates **Ingredients:** 250 grams of net melon, 100 grams of Parma ham **Preparation:** Cut the melon into slices and serve with the Parma ham. This combination goes perfectly together and ensures a good start to the day.

Delicious cheese and spinach omelette

313.6 kcal | 29.1 grams of protein | 20 grams of fat | 2.8 grams of carbohydrates **Ingredients:** 2 eggs, 60 grams of grated cheese, 50 grams of spinach leaves, 1 teaspoon of oil, 1 tablespoon of crème fraîche, Himalayan salt and pepper **Preparation:** Put the oil in a pan and fry the eggs together with the cheese in the pan . Then add the spinach leaves and turn the omelette as soon as it starts to thicken. Finally, add the crème fraîche to the omelette, season and serve.

Hearty breakfast soup the Asian way

105.2 kcal | 8.9 grams of protein | 0.7 grams of fat | 12.6 grams of carbohydrates **Ingredients:** 200 ml of vegetable stock, 3 prawns, 30 grams of bean sprouts, 30 grams of bamboo shoots, 10 grams of glass noodles, a small piece of fresh ginger, a chilli pepper, sharp fish sauce and fresh coriander to sprinkle. **Preparation:** Put the vegetable stock in a saucepan and simmer together with the grated ginger and chili peppers. Next, add the prawns and let them cook. Now let the glass noodles soak in hot water for about 5 minutes and then add them to the saucepan with the stock and the prawns. Then add the bamboo shoots and season everything with the fish sauce. Finally, sprinkle the soup with the coriander and serve.

Cream cheese with a crunchy apple

139.4 kcal | 10.8 grams of protein | 3.4 grams of fat | 15.8 grams of carbohydrates **Ingredients:** 1 apple, 1 chilli pepper, 1 tablespoon of vegetable oil, 1 clove of garlic, 100 grams of grainy cream cheese, juice of a lime, 10 grams of coriander, 1 pinch of Himalayan salt **Preparation:** the chilli, coriander, garlic, salt and lime juice in a mortar or mix in a blender. Then remove the pips from the apple and cut it into thin slices. The apple slices are then fried in a pan with a little oil and then coated with the marinade. Arrange with the grainy cream cheese before serving.

Hearty ham salad

234.3 kcal | 29 grams of protein | 4.9 grams of fat | 17.4 grams of carbohydrates **Ingredients:** 50 grams of quark, 50 grams of grainy cream cheese, 80 grams of turkey ham, 1 tomato, 1/2 yellow pepper, 1 pickle, 1/2 apple, 2 tablespoons raspberry vinegar, 1 tablespoon herbs, Himalayan salt, Pepper **Preparation:** Cut the ham, tomato, bell pepper, pickled cucumber and apple into cubes and then mix with the quark and cream cheese. Finally add the herbs and vinegar and season with salt and pepper. The salad goes perfectly with a slice of protein bread. However, this was not included in the nutritional table.

Omelette with tomato juice

249 kcal | 20.5 grams of protein | 17 grams of fat | 3.5 grams of carbohydrates **Ingredients:** 2 eggs, 50 ml of tomato juice, 1/2 bunch

of basil, Himalayan salt, pepper, 1 tablespoon of grated Parmesan **Preparation:** Put the eggs and tomato juice together and mix. This now put them in a pan and fry briefly. Then season the omelette with salt and pepper and sprinkle with herbs and cheese for perfect enjoyment.

Pancakes with fruity berries

424.6 kcal | 32.8 grams of protein | 25.2 grams of fat | 11.1 grams of carbohydrates **Ingredients:** 50 ml coconut milk, 50 ml mineral water, 2 eggs, 50 grams almond flour, 1/2 teaspoon baking powder, 100 grams fresh or frozen berry mix, 1 teaspoon xylitol **Preparation:** The coconut milk, the water, the eggs, the Mix the flour and baking powder into a pancake batter. Then bake the pancakes in a pan until golden yellow on both sides. At the same time, mix the berries with the xylitol with a hand blender or in a blender. Now serve the pancakes with the berry puree.

Breakfast waffles

430 kcal | 36 grams of protein | 19.3 grams of fat | 33.3 grams of carbohydrates **Ingredients:** 250 grams of yoghurt, 2 eggs, 1 teaspoon of baking powder, 30 grams of almond flour, 1 tablespoon of xylitol **Preparation:** Mix all ingredients into a dough and pour into the muffin tins. Silicone molds are best for this as the dough is less likely to stick in shape. Then bake for 20 minutes at 170 degrees. The recipe makes about four muffins.

Fit into the day with pomelo, oranges and grapefruit

112 kcal | 2.6 grams of protein | 0.4 grams of fat | 24 grams of carbohydrates **Ingredients:** 100 grams of pomelo, 1 orange and 1 grapefruit **Preparation:** A special energy kick for breakfast. Gentle on the stomach and sufficient in vitamin C.

Mushroom omlette

196.4 kcal | 13.9 grams of protein | 14.5 grams of fat | 2.8 grams of carbohydrates **Ingredients:** 80 grams of chanterelles, 1 shallot, 1 sprig of thyme, 1 tablespoon of yogurt, 2 eggs, 1 tablespoon of butter **Preparation:** Fry the diced shallots with the chanterelles in the butter. Mix the yogurt and thyme leaves together with the eggs and pour over the chanterelles. Let the whole thing stand briefly on low heat and bake to the end.

Protein bread served with smoked salmon and cream horseradish

321.6 kcal | 31.2 grams of protein | 22.9 grams of fat | 7.2 grams of carbohydrates

Ingredients: 1 tablespoon of grated horseradish, 100 grams of smoked salmon, 2 tablespoons of Greek yogurt, 2 slices of protein bread, Himalayan salt, pepper

Preparation: Stir the horseradish into the yogurt and then let it steep. A pinch of salt and pepper to taste the salmon and you're done. Now grill the bread in the toaster and arrange everything. Good Appetite.

Delicious coconut rolls

One bun has: 308 kcal | 12.6 grams of protein | 21.4 grams of fat | 17 grams of carbohydrates **Ingredients:** 100 grams of butter, 100 grams of coconut fat, 500 grams of quark, 6 eggs, 6 tablespoons of xylitol, 100 grams of almond flour, 100 grams of coconut flour, 100 grams of coconut flakes, 1 tablespoon of baking powder

Preparation:
Mix the quark, eggs, butter and coconut fat to a smooth mass. Now mix in the remaining ingredients and form about 12 small piles. Then place them on the baking sheet with sufficient space between them. It is advisable to prepare a larger amount and freeze it. Now bake in the oven at 175 degrees for 30 minutes and you're done.

Nut rolls with apple pieces

One bun has: 315 kcal | 26.8 grams of protein | 17.9 grams of fat | 9.2 grams of carbohydrates **Ingredients:** 500 grams of quark, 6 eggs, 100 grams of almond flour, 100 grams of coconut flour, 100 grams of walnuts, 3 apples (300 grams), 1 tablespoon of baking powder **Preparation:** Cut the pitted and peeled apples into cubes. Mix the remaining ingredients together with the walnuts, chopped beforehand. Moisten your hands and form small rolls from the apples and the other ingredients. Quantities for approx. 8 rolls. Then put the whole thing in the oven for 30 minutes at 170 degrees. They are particularly easy to keep fresh in the freezer but also in the refrigerator. Quickly baked again in the oven before consumption, the rolls are twice as enjoyable.

A special kind of scrambled eggs - with crabs

321 kcal | 25.5 grams of protein | 17.9 grams of fat | 11.7 grams of carbohydrates **Ingredients:** 2 eggs, 50 grams of fresh or frozen crabs, 1/2 red bell pepper, 1/2 yellow bell pepper, 2 shallots, 1 clove of garlic, chives to sprinkle, coconut oil for the pan **Preparation:** Chop the garlic and shallots and fry in coconut oil. Add the peppers together with the crabs and let cook. Beat the eggs and pour over them. Divide

the whole thing in the pan and let it fry well. If necessary, then sprinkle with fresh and tasty herbs. This individually increases the taste and goes perfectly with the scrambled crab eggs.

LIGHT AND TASTY RECIPES FOR LUNCH

The following recipes for lunch are fixed, they taste absolutely delicious and are healthy and do not burden the body. Lunch is often skipped, especially when working, because heavy dishes often make you tired.

With these recipes, however, you can continue with your usual daily routine satisfied and with a lot of vigor. The dishes for morning, noon and evening should only give you a guideline. You can of course design the menu as you wish.

Smoked trout fillet with fresh fennel salad and delicious wasabi dip

239.3 kcal | Protein: 28.3 grams | Fat: 10.9 grams | Carbohydrates: 7 grams **Preparation time:** 10 minutes **Ingredients:** 120 grams of smoked trout | 1/2 tuber of fennel | 1 orange filleted | 1 pinch of cardamom | 1/2 teaspoon dill chopped | 1 tsp walnut oil | Himalayan salt and pepper | 2 tbsp sour cream | 1 splash of lime juice | 1/2 pinch of wasabi paste **Preparation:** Grate the fennel finely and the orange into pieces. Then both ingredients can be mixed together. Now season this with cardamom, dill, walnut oil, salt and pepper. Mix the sour cream with the lime juice and the wasabi paste. You can also use horseradish here. Finally, the trout can be served with the salad and the dip.

Fried pumpkin with creamed spinach

292.6 kcal | Protein: 8.7 grams | Fat: 24.2 grams | Carbohydrates: 10.6 grams

Preparation time: 23 minutes

Ingredients: 80 grams of spinach leaves | 1/2 red onion | 1 clove of garlic | 1 teaspoon butter | 50 ml cream | 1 tbsp cottage cheese

| Himalayan salt and pepper | some nutmeg grated | 80 grams of Hokkaido pumpkin | 1 teaspoon olive oil | 1/2 teaspoon rosemary chopped | 1 teaspoon of pumpkin seeds roasted and chopped

Preparation:

Chop the onion and garlic and sweat everything in butter until translucent. Now the cream can be added and the cottage cheese can be stirred in. Add the spinach leaves and simmer for 2 minutes. Next, season with salt, pepper and nutmeg and remove from the heat. Peel the pumpkin and cut it into pieces 1/2 cm thick. Fry these in a little olive oil until golden brown on all sides, season with salt, pepper and rosemary and serve with the spinach. Finally, generously sprinkle everything with the chopped and roasted pumpkin seeds.

Curry minute steaks

346 kcal | Protein: 39.8 grams | Fat: 20.4 grams | Carbohydrates: 0.8 grams

Preparation time: 12 minutes

Ingredients: 140 grams of minute steaks, (pork, beef or poultry) | 1/2 teaspoon olive oil | 1/2 teaspoon curry paste red from the Asia store | 1 egg | 1 tbsp Parmesan finely grated **Preparation:** Mix the olive oil with the red curry paste and brush the meat with it. This can then be seared in a grill pan without fat on both sides for one minute on a high heat. Now fry a fried egg, which can then be sprinkled with parmesan and served with the meat. A small leaf salad with a dressing of yogurt and lemon juice can also be served to go with it.

Greek-style vegetable stir-fry with raw lamb ham

297.9 kcal | Protein: 17.5 grams | Fat: 21.5 grams | Carbohydrates: 8.9 grams

Preparation time: 20 minutes

Ingredients: 1/2 zucchini | 1/4 yellow pepper | 1/4 red pepper | 1/4 eggplant | 1/2 red onion | 2 tomatoes | 1 tbsp olive oil | Thyme | Himalayan salt and pepper | 50 grams of sheep's cheese, firm | 30 grams of lamb ham thinly sliced

Preparation:
Cut the courgette, bell pepper, aubergine, onion and tomato into 1 cm cubes. Then roast everything in olive oil for about 10 minutes. Keep stirring the vegetables so that they don't get too dark. Season the whole thing with salt and pepper and then flavor everything with thyme. Arrange the dish on a plate and crumble the sheep's cheese over it. Finally, the lamb ham can be draped over it.

Filled Toscana zucchini

149.5 kcal | Protein: 7 grams | Fat: 5.5 grams | Carbohydrates: 18 grams

Preparation time: 23 minutes

Ingredients: 1 zucchini | 1 shallot | 60 grams of cherry tomatoes | 1 fig | 1/2 pear | 8 black or green olives | Himalayan salt and pepper | Fresh or dried basil | 2 tbsp Parmesan

Preparation:
Cut the zucchini lengthways and scrape out the core with a spoon. Now shallots, cherry tomatoes, figs and pears can be cut into small pieces and mixed together. Then season the whole thing with salt and pepper and fill the zucchini with it. Lightly press the olives into the filling and sprinkle everything with the basil. Finally, the parmesan can be spread over it and the zucchini can be placed on a baking sheet lined with baking paper. Finally, bake the filled zucchini in the oven at 200 ° Celsius for 15 minutes on top and bottom heat.

Konjac pasta salad

318 kcal | Protein: 19.6 grams | Fat: 21.2 grams | Carbohydrates: 12.2 grams **Preparation time:** 15 minutes **Ingredients:** 50 grams of konjac noodles | 1/4 green pepper | 1/2 yellow pepper | 1/2 apple red | 1/2 cucumber | 20 grams of turkey ham diced | 1 tbsp walnuts chopped | 20 grams of sliced cheese, diced | 1/2 chicory red | Juice and zest of half an untreated organic lemon | 1 tbsp sour cream | Himalayan salt and pepper | 1 tbsp chives chopped | 1 teaspoon chervil, chopped **Preparation:** Rinse the konjac noodles and briefly boil them. Now quench with cold water and set aside. First mix the juice and zest of the lemon with the sour cream and then mix the cream with chives and chervil. Salt and pepper well. Finely dice the peppers and coarsely grate the apple and cucumber. Then cut the chicory into strips and stir everything together with the diced turkey ham. Mix in the walnuts and cheese. Now the konjac noodles can be folded in and mixed with the prepared marinade. Finally, season to taste and enjoy.

Turkey steak with a delicious herb and cream cheese sauce

231.6 kcal | Protein: 36.9 grams | Fat: 7.2 grams | Carbohydrates: 4.8 grams **Preparation time:** 16 minutes **Ingredients:** 150 grams turkey steak | 1 shallot | 1 clove of garlic | 1 teaspoon butter | 1 tbsp lemon juice | 80 ml of broth | 1 tbsp cream cheese | 1/2 teaspoon chopped parsley | 1/2 teaspoon chopped tarragon | 1/2 teaspoon chopped coriander | Himalayan salt | white pepper **Preparation:** Salt and pepper the meat and then fry it in a grill pan without fat on both sides for two minutes each. Now cut the shallot and the garlic into small pieces and sweat them lightly in the butter. First, the whole thing is deglazed with the lemon juice and poured over with the broth. Bring this to the boil briefly and then stir in the cream cheese with a whisk. First, the sauce can be removed from the flame and the herbs can be stirred in. Finally, season to taste with salt and pepper, briefly place the meat in the sauce, leave to stand for a minute and serve.

Exotic chicken curry with papaya and mango

317 kcal | Protein: 42.9 grams | Fat: 10.2 grams | Carbohydrates: 13.4 grams **Preparation time:** 14 minutes **Ingredients:** 130 grams of skinless chicken breast | 1/2 red onion | 1 tbsp vegetable oil | 1/2 teaspoon curry powder yellow | Juice of half a lime | 1/2 stick of celery | 1/2 mango | 50 grams of papaya | 80 ml of broth | 3 tbsp yogurt | 1 red chilli | some Himalayan salt | 1 tbsp chopped coriander **Preparation:** Cut the chicken into thin strips and the onion into fine cubes. Sear the whole thing in oil for two minutes. Then sprinkle everything with the curry powder and let it roast briefly. Now deglaze with the lime juice and add the broth directly. Next, cut the celery, mango and papaya into 1 cm cubes and add these to the pan as well. Chop the chilli and mix this with the yogurt. Now stir the spicy yogurt into the broth. Add a little more salt to the whole thing. Before serving, you can generously sprinkle the dish with chopped coriander.

Paprika strips with delicious chicken breast

263.1 kcal | Protein: 47.1 grams | Fat: 5.1 grams | Carbohydrates: 7.2 grams

Preparation time: 22 minutes

Ingredients: 140 grams of skinless chicken breast | Himalayan salt and pepper | Mild paprika powder | 1/4 red pepper | 1/4 yellow pepper | 1/4 green pepper | 1/2 red onion | 1 tbsp cream cheese | 2 sprigs of thyme **Preparation:** Cut the chicken breast into three equal pieces and rub them with salt, pepper and paprika powder. First cut the bell pepper and onion into strips, mix everything together and put them together in a small baking dish. Season the whole thing with salt and pepper and then flavor it with thyme. Place the chicken breast on top and spread the cream cheese over the chicken breast. The whole thing can now be baked in the oven for 15 minutes at 180 ° Celsius (convection). Finally, take the dish out of the oven, arrange on a plate and enjoy.

Camembert coated with bacon

708.6 kcal | Protein: 56.5 grams | Fat: 51.8 grams | Carbohydrates: 4.8 grams

Preparation time: 12 minutes

Ingredients: 1 Camembert with about 125 grams | 6 thin slices of pork belly or bacon | 1 pinch of hot paprika powder | 1 tbsp almond flour | 1 egg | 2 tbsp low-fat milk | 4 tbsp finely grated almonds | 1 teaspoon of chopped rosemary

Preparation:

Rub the camembert with the paprika powder, then wrap it with the bacon and finally roll it in the almond flour. Whisk the egg with the low-fat milk and pull the cheese through. Mix grated almonds with rosemary and bread the camembert in it. Now pull the cheese through the egg one more time and bread it again. Place the Camembert on the grill rack and heat the oven to 200 ° Celsius. The whole thing can be baked for 7 minutes in a fan oven.

Delicious pollack in a curry sauce on cherry tomatoes

289.8 kcal | Protein: 27.9 grams | Fat: 17.5 grams | Carbohydrates: 5.4 grams **Preparation time:** 18 minutes **Ingredients:** 130 grams of saithe filleted | 1 shallot | 1 clove of garlic | 1/2 teaspoon vegetable oil | 1/2 teaspoon curry powder yellow | 2 allspice grains | 2 cloves | 2 cardamom pods | 1 stick of celery | 1 tomato | 500 ml broth | 2 spring onions | Himalayan salt and pepper **Preparation:** At the beginning, finely chop the shallot and the clove of garlic and lightly roast this together with the curry powder in oil. Then add the allspice, cloves and cardamom and pour the broth on top. Now let it boil briefly. Next, cut the celery and tomatoes into small pieces and add everything to the stock along with the fish. First season with salt and pepper and simmer over medium heat for 12 minutes. Chop the spring onions and remove the fish and vegetables from the stock. Now serve the vegetables and fish with a little liquid and sprinkle with spring onions. You can store the rest of the brew in the refrigerator or freeze it.

Fine smoked salmon frittata with fresh dill

442.9 kcal | Protein: 40.3 grams | Fat: 29.7 grams | Carbohydrates: 3.6 grams

Preparation time: 20 minutes

Ingredients: 2 eggs | 60 ml buttermilk | 100 grams of smoked salmon | Juice and zest of half an untreated organic lemon | Himalayan salt and pepper | 1 tbsp dill chopped | 20 grams of grated butter cheese

Preparation:
Whisk the eggs with the buttermilk and add the juice and zest of the

lemon. Now season with salt, pepper and dill. Then pour the eggs into a round tart pan and spread the coarsely chopped smoked salmon on top. Now sprinkle everything with the butter cheese and heat the oven to 190 ° Celsius. Let the frittata bake on top and bottom heat for 15 minutes. A small mixed salad can be served to go with it. You can marinate this with a little apple cider vinegar and olive oil.

Spicy sausage salad with radishes, chilli and coriander

191.1 kcal | Protein: 10.8 grams | Fat: 7.9 grams | Carbohydrates: 19.2 grams

Preparation time: 10 minutes

Ingredients: 100 grams of poultry sausage | 3 radishes | 2 gherkins with no added sugar | 1 red chilli | 1/4 red pepper | 1/2 chicory | 1/2 bunch of coriander chopped | 1 tomato | Himalayan salt | 2 tbsp apple cider vinegar | 4 tbsp water or broth | 1 tbsp vegetable oil

Preparation:
At the beginning cut the poultry sausage into thin strips, the radishes and pickles into slices and the chilli, paprika, chicory and tomatoes into cubes. Mix everything together with the chopped

coriander. Apple cider vinegar, water and oil can now be mixed into a marinade. Lightly salt these and use them to dress the sausage salad.

Vegetable thalers baked with cheese and bacon

390.1 kcal | Protein: 23.3 grams | Fat: 27.7 grams | Carbohydrates: 11.9 grams

Preparation time: 20 minutes **Ingredients:** 1/2 zucchini | 1/4 carrot | 20 grams of celeriac | 1 teaspoon sesame seeds | 1 egg | 2 tbsp oat bran | 1 tbsp grated almonds | 1 teaspoon parsley chopped | Himalayan salt and pepper | 1/2 teaspoon lovage chopped | 20 grams of bacon diced | 2 tbsp grated mountain cheese | some marjoram **Preparation:** Grate the zucchini, carrot and celery very finely. Then mix this with the sesame, egg, oat bran and almonds. First mix in the parsley and lovage and season with salt and pepper. Thaler can now be formed from this mass. I do this best with wet hands. Fry the thalers in a coated pan for 2 minutes on each side. Mix the bacon with mountain cheese and marjoram and cover the thalers with it. These can now be placed on a baking sheet lined with baking paper. If the grill function is used, gratinate for about 3 minutes.

Delicious chicken caprese

368.9 kcal | Protein: 52.1 grams | Fat: 16.5 grams | Carbohydrates: 3 grams

Preparation time: 20 minutes

Ingredients: 130 grams of skinless chicken breast | 1 tbsp olive oil | some zest of an untreated organic lemon | 1/2 bunch of basil | Himalayan salt and pepper | 1/2 tomato | 1/2 scoop of mozzarella

Preparation:
Salt and pepper the chicken. Then mix the olive oil with the lemon zest and the basil in a blender to make a pesto. Now salt and pepper this and brush the chicken breast with it. Cut the chicken breast deeply at the top and cut the tomato and mozzarella into slices. First, insert the tomato and mozzarella into the notches on the chicken. Place the chicken on a baking sheet lined with baking paper and let it cook at 180 ° Celsius for 12 minutes on top and bottom heat.

Fresh asparagus in baked ham and cheese rolls

560 kcal | Protein: 37.3 grams | Fat: 38.4 grams | Carbohydrates: 16.3 grams

Preparation time: 16 minutes

Ingredients: 8 slices of turkey ham | 4 slices of Gouda cheese | 2 stalks of green asparagus | 1 tbsp almond flour | 1 tbsp low-fat milk | 2 tbsp walnuts finely grated | Himalayan salt and pepper | 1 tbsp sour cream | 1/2 teaspoon mustard without added sugar

Preparation:
Place two slices of ham on top of each other and cover them with a slice of cheese. Cut the asparagus in half and place it on top of the cheese. Now the whole thing can be rolled up and rolled in almond flour. Then whisk the egg with the milk and pull the rolls through. Now bread the coated asparagus in the walnuts and place them on a baking sheet lined with baking paper. Bake the rolls at 180 ° Celsius and convection for 6 minutes. Mix sour cream, mustard, salt and pepper to make a dip and serve it with the rolls.

Almond bonnet meets ostrich steak

370 kcal | 30.2 grams of protein | 23.3 grams of fat | 7.2 grams of

carbohydrates **Ingredients:** 180 grams of steak from the ostrich, 1 clove of garlic, 3 tablespoons of almond sticks, 1 tablespoon of parsley finely chopped, 2 cherry tomatoes, 1/4 yellow pepper, Himalayan salt, pepper, 1 tablespoon of parmesan, oil for frying **Preparation:** First, salt and pepper the meat. Sear it in the pan and then take it out. Now the almonds, parsley, parmesan and garlic are pressed. In addition, there are chopped peppers and finely chopped tomatoes. Mix the mixture and season with salt and pepper. Spread this on the meat and bake it in the oven at 150 ° Celsius for 15 minutes.

Crispy roast duck

399.6 kcal | 32 grams of protein | 26.2 grams of fat | 6 grams of carbohydrates

Ingredients: 180 grams of duck breast, Himalayan salt, pepper, soy sauce, 1 clove of garlic, 150 grams of bean sprouts, 1 tablespoon of coriander, 1 tablespoon of chopped spring onions, oil for frying

Preparation:
First, the duck breast is rubbed with salt, pepper and soy sauce and

about marinated for half an hour. Fry the duck skin side down in a pan without fat. This is then cooked in the oven at 130 ° Celsius for 25 minutes. Now roast the garlic in the same pan and extinguish it with 3 tablespoons of water. Now season the whole thing with soy sauce and toss the bean sprouts in it. Mix in the coriander and spring onion. Then fry the duck for 3 minutes in 180 ° Celsius hot fat. Take the duck out of the fat, let it drain very well and then pat it dry. Cut the duck into thin slices and arrange them on the sprouts. Sprinkle with chopped peanuts and chilli if necessary.

Tasty sweet potatoes with kangaroo

519.2 kcal | 33.9 grams of protein | 29.6 grams of fat | 22 grams of carbohydrates **Ingredients:** 180 grams of kangaroo steak, 1 sweet potato, 150 ml of coconut milk, 1 tablespoon of desiccated coconut, thyme, Himalayan salt, pepper, 1 tablespoon of chilli oil for frying, 1 stick of lemongrass **Preparation:** Salt and pepper the steak and fry it in the chilli oil for about 3 minutes on each side. Now free the sweet potatoes from their peel and toss them very finely. Now the coconut milk is flavored with the lemongrass and the thyme and the sweet potato is cooked in it. After about 15 minutes, add the desiccated coconut and let it simmer briefly. The whole thing can now be seasoned with salt and pepper. Before serving, pour the potato cream over the meat in the pan and let it steep for a moment.

Delicious goose breast prepared in a Roman pot

502.1 kcal | 21 grams of protein | 40.1 grams of fat | 11.6 grams of carbohydrates **Ingredients:** 200 grams of goose breast, 1/2 organic orange, 1/2 apple, 30 grams of celery, 1 shallot, rosemary, thyme, 200 ml of broth, 100 grams of pumpkin, Himalayan salt, pepper **Preparation:** Grate the Mix the goose breast with salt and pepper. First the orange must be filleted, the shallot finely chopped, the apple diced, the celery and pumpkin cut into bite-sized pieces. Put everything in the Römertopf together with the herbs. Cover this with the broth and place the goose breast skin-side up on top. Now only the Roman pot needs to be closed. Let the dish simmer in the oven at 160 ° Celsius for one hour. Now you can eat.

Hearty Swedish meatballs

Preparation time: 6 minutes Cooking time: 15 minutes

404 kcal | Protein: 30.5 grams | Fat: 29.6 grams | Carbohydrates: 3.9 grams

Ingredients:

For the balls: 100 grams of ground beef, 1 tablespoon of chopped shallots, 2 tablespoons of milk, 1 egg, 2 tablespoons of almond flour, 1 pinch of hot mustard, salt and pepper, 1 teaspoon of oil

For the sauce: 6 grams Butter, 6 grams of almond flour, 100 ml of stock, 50 ml of cream, soy sauce and pepper

Preparation:

For the meatballs, knead all the ingredients together and shape them into balls with wet hands. Then fry them in a little oil on all sides for about 8 minutes. For the sauce, melt the butter and stir in the almond flour. Let the whole thing roast lightly while stirring constantly. Pour everything up with the broth. Stir until the sauce comes to a boil. Refine the sauce with the cream. Now this can be seasoned with soy sauce and pepper and the balls can be added. Briefly toss the meatballs in the sauce.

DISHES WITH CHICKEN

Spicy Iberian chicken with delicious crayfish

371.8 kcal | 42.2 grams of protein | 15.4 grams of fat | 8.3 grams of carbohydrates **Ingredients:** 100 grams of chicken breast, 20 grams of crayfish, 1 tbsp piri piri paste (aromatic pepper paste from Portugal), 1/4 red bell pepper, 1/4 yellow bell pepper, 1/2 zucchini, 100 grams parsley root, 1 shallot , 2 cloves of garlic, rosemary, thyme, lavender, Himalayan salt, peppercorns, 4 black olives without a core, 150 ml stock, 2 tablespoons olive oil **Preparation:** Preheat the oven to 180 ° Celsius. Mix the oil with the piri piri paste and marinate the chicken with it. Then let it soak in for 10 minutes. Cut the vegetables into bite-sized pieces. Peel and quarter the shallot, peel the garlic and use it whole. Now take an ovenproof baking dish and create a nice bed with half of the vegetables. Now place the chicken on top and cover it with the remaining vegetables, crayfish and herbs. Season with salt and pepper and carefully pour the broth over it. Finally let it stew in the oven for about 35 minutes.

Delicious Thai coconut chicken

272 kcal | 21 grams of protein | 17.2 grams of fat | 9.2 grams of carbohydrates **Ingredients:** 130 grams of chicken breast, 1 tomato, 1 chilli pepper, 30 grams of mushrooms, 1 lemongrass, ginger or galangal, lime leaves (called kaffir lime leaves), juice of an organic lime, 100 ml of coconut milk, 100 ml of broth, a Sprinkle of fish sauce, a dash of soy sauce, 1 clove of garlic, if necessary a dash of sweetener **Preparation:** Heat the coconut milk with the broth and flavor with the lime leaves, lemongrass and ginger or galangal, garlic and chili peppers. Now cut the mushrooms, tomatoes and chicken breast into bite-sized pieces and add them to the stock. Then season with the soy sauce and the fish sauce and add a little sweetener to taste. After about 10 minutes of cooking it is ready and you can enjoy it.

Hearty Szeged goulash with delicious chicken

205.4 kcal | 33.6 grams of protein | 3.6 grams of fat | 7.2 grams of carbohydrates **Ingredients:** 130 grams of chicken breast, 1 onion, 1 clove of garlic, 1 tablespoon of sweet paprika, 1 teaspoon of tomato paste, oil for frying, thyme, marjoram, 1 bay leaf, 100 grams of sauerkraut, 150 ml stock, Himalayan salt, pepper, 1 pinch of ground caraway seeds 1/2 potato, 2 tbsp sour cream

Preparation:

Cut the meat into 3 cm pieces. Fry with a little hot oil and then remove from the pan. Now the onions and garlic will sweat until golden brown. Roast the tomato paste and paprika powder and pour in the broth. Now season with the bay leaf, caraway seeds, salt, pepper and thyme. Now add the sauerkraut and the meat. Let simmer on low heat for about 45 minutes. Rub the potato very finely into the goulash. This makes the goulash nice and creamy. Serve this delicious Hungarian favorite dish with two tablespoons of sour cream to refine it.

Crunchy green beans with chicken breast in a creamy pepper sauce

323.2 kcal | 44 grams of protein | 10.9 grams of fat | 9.4 grams of carbohydrates **Ingredients:** 130 grams of chicken breast, 1/2 onion, 50 ml of cream, 50 ml of broth, 1 tablespoon of green peppercorns, (from the jar), Himalayan salt, pepper, 100 grams of green beans, 2 slices of bacon, 1 Teaspoon of savory, 1 clove of garlic, oil for frying **Preparation:** Season the chicken breast with salt and pepper and fry it on both sides in a little oil. Now cook for 15 minutes in the oven at 120 ° Celsius. Finely chop the onion and garlic and roast in the same pan. Pour the broth over it and add the peppercorns and cream. Let something boil. Free the beans from the hard ends and peel off the fibers. Briefly blanch the beans and cut in half. Cut the bacon into fine cubes and leave in the pan. Add the beans and stir well. Season with salt, pepper and savory. Serve the chicken breast with the sauce and beans.

Delicious Swiss chard with chicken breast

228.6 kcal | 42.4 grams of protein | 4.7 grams of fat | 1.3 grams of carbohydrates **Ingredients:** 130 grams of chicken breast, 1 red onion, 60 grams of oyster mushrooms, 1 teaspoon of Indian curry powder, 1 clove of garlic, zest of an organic orange, 100 grams of Swiss chard, 50 ml of broth, 1 teaspoon of cold butter, some oil for frying, Himalayan salt, pepper **Preparation:** Marinate the chicken breast with the zest of the organic orange, salt and pepper. Now fry the chicken in a little oil, then cook over a low heat for 10 minutes while turning several times. Cut the onion and garlic into small pieces and then sauté in the pan. Now pluck the oyster mushrooms into bite-sized pieces and cut the chard into large pieces. Now add it to the onion in the pan and dust it with yellow curry powder. Pour in the broth as well. Simmer for about 3 minutes and season with salt and pepper. Finally add the cold butter and enjoy.

DISHES WITH TURKEY

Turkey schnitzel filled with mozzarella and tomato

298 kcal | 44 grams of protein | 13 grams of fat | 1.5 grams of carbohydrates **Ingredients:** 150 grams of turkey escalope, 1/2 scoop of mozzarella, 1/2 tomato, 2 sage leaves, 2 basil leaves, Himalayan salt, pepper, 1 clove of garlic, 1 tablespoon soy sauce, oil for frying, toothpick to fix **Preparation:** Cover Cover the turkey escalope with cling film and then pound it thinly. Cut the tomato and mozzarella into thin slices. Cover half of the schnitzel alternately with tomato and mozzarella. Now place the herbs on top and close the schnitzel. Fix the two ends with a toothpick. Now finely chop the garlic and mix it with the soy sauce, then brush the schnitzel with it. Then fry it in a pan with a little oil. Cook at 150 ° Celsius in the oven for 10 minutes. If necessary, season with salt and pepper and serve.

Golden turkey nuggets

492.9 kcal | 56.6 grams of protein | 19.9 grams of fat | 21.2 grams of carbohydrates **Ingredients:** 130 grams of turkey, 1 egg, 2 tablespoons of almond flour, 100 ml of soy milk, Himalayan salt, pepper, zest of an organic lemon, 1 tablespoon of parsley, oil for deep-frying **Preparation:** Separate the egg and beat the egg white a stiff snow. Now stir together the yolk, the milk, the zest of the lemon, the parsley and the almond flour. Now season with salt and pepper and carefully fold in the egg whites. Cut the turkey into strips. Then pull the strips through the dough and fry it in hot oil. Finally, drain well and dab off.

Turkey with a difference (Mexican style)

320.2 kcal | 41 grams of protein | 9.3 grams of fat | 15 grams of carbohydrates **Ingredients:** 130 grams of turkey, 1 tomato, 1/2 red pepper, 1/2 yellow pepper, 1 tablespoon tomato paste, 50 grams of corn, 50 grams of red beans, 2 chili peppers, 1 tablespoon of sour cream, 1 tablespoon of parmesan, Himalayan salt , Pepper, 1 clove of garlic, 1 red onion, 1 teaspoon sweet paprika, marjoram, thyme, 100 ml stock **Preparation:** Cut the meat into small cubes and fry it in a non-stick pan. Add the finely chopped onion and garlic and roast. Also briefly toast the tomato paste and paprika powder and add the broth. Now the peppers are diced, chopped chilli and added with the corn and beans. Season with salt and pepper and add the herbs. Finally simmer for about 30 minutes on a low heat. Refine with the sour cream and parmesan and serve.

Turkey Masala (Indian style)

238.6 kcal | 35.7 grams of protein | 6.1 grams of fat | 10 grams of carbohydrates **Ingredients:** 130 grams of turkey, 1 tablespoon of spice mix for Tikka Masala, 100 grams of yogurt, 1 cardamom capsule, 1/2 teaspoon of cumin, 1/2 teaspoon of freshly grated ginger, 1 clove of garlic, 1 small shallot, juice of an organic lemon, 1/2 red paprika, Himalayan salt, pepper, 1 teaspoon tomato paste, oil for frying, 100 ml stock **Preparation:** Cut the meat into 2 cm pieces and fry it in a pan with a little oil. Add the shallot and garlic, chopped beforehand, to the meat. Also add the tomato paste to the pan and roast lightly. Now add the broth. Mix the yogurt with the spice mixture, the crushed cardamom capsule, the caraway seeds, the ginger and the lemon juice. Let the meat simmer for 15 minutes and then add the yoghurt to the pan. Finally, the peppers are finely diced and also put in the pan. After another 10 minutes you can serve it up and enjoy.

Turkey with delicious cream pumpkin

297.2 kcal | 32.6 grams of protein | 12.7 grams of fat | 14.4 grams of carbohydrates **Ingredients:** 130 grams of turkey, 100 grams of pumpkin (preferably butternut squash), 1 clove of garlic, 1 shallot, juice of an organic lemon, 50 ml of cream, Himalayan salt, pepper, 1/2 teaspoon of ginger, thyme, oil for searing **Preparation:** First the turkey is pounded thinly, then salted and peppered and fried in a coated pan. Now take a second pan and add the diced shallot and the finely chopped garlic with a little oil, sweat until translucent. Now cut the pumpkin into pieces about 1 cm in size and add it to the pan with the onion. Season with thyme, ginger, salt and pepper and pour the cream and lemon juice over it. Arrange the squash in a deep plate and place the meat on top. Do you enjoy your delicious natural turkeys ??

PIG DISHES

Pork fillet medallions with delicious cinnamon plum sauce

303.6 kcal | 31.4 grams of protein | 12.4 grams of fat | 16 grams of carbohydrates **Ingredients:** 150 grams of pork tenderloin, 50 grams of plums, 1 clove of garlic, 1 shallot, 75 ml of vegetable stock, Himalayan salt, pepper, 1/2 cinnamon stick, 1 pinch of star anise, thyme, rosemary, a little oil, 2 tablespoons of butter **Preparation:** Season Cook the meat whole with salt and pepper and only then cut it into medallions. Put some oil in a pan and fry it, do not fry it through. Now put the medallions in the oven at 100 ° Celsius for 12 minutes. Now cut the shallot and garlic finely and sweat it with the roast residue. Core and cut the plums into small pieces and then add them to the pan. Now pour the stock over it and add the thyme, star anise, cinnamon stick and the rosemary. Bring to the boil once and simmer over low heat until it is slightly reduced. Then add the butter and melt it down. The medallions can now be served with the sauce. Enjoy your meal

Curry with pork and green peas (Thai style)

332.8 kcal | 27.7 grams of protein | 18.3 grams of fat | 8.6 grams of carbohydrates **Ingredients:** 140 grams of pork tenderloin, 1 tablespoon of green curry paste, 50 grams of peas, 50 grams of eggplant, 50 grams of zucchini, 100 ml of coconut milk, 100 ml of broth, soy sauce and fish sauce. **Preparation:** Toast the curry paste without oil in a coated pan and then add the pork fillet cut into small cubes. Also add the chopped aubergines and zucchini to the pan. Now pour the whole thing up with the broth and stir it until all of the green curry paste dissolves. Finally add the peas and coconut milk and season with the fish and soy sauce.

Nürnberger Schweins-Schäufele

306.9 kcal | 24 grams of protein | 22.5 grams of fat | 2 grams of carbohydrates **Ingredients:** 500 grams of pork shovel with bones, 150 grams of root vegetables consisting of leek, celery, carrot, onion, rosemary, thyme, 1/2 teaspoon of tomato paste, 1/2 teaspoon of ground caraway, 2 juniper berries, 1 bay leaf, 2 Garlic cloves, 200 ml stock, Himalayan salt, pepper **Preparation:** Cut a diamond shape into the rind of the meat. Salt and pepper the meat, then rub it in well. So that the fat separates from the meat, sear the rind side in a pan without oil or fat. Now fry on all sides and remove from the pan. Roughly cut the root vegetables and roast them in the drained fat. Then add tomato paste and roast. Now deglaze with the broth and add the spices, herbs and garlic. Put everything in a baking dish, place the bone side of the meat on top. Cook in the oven at 170 ° Celsius for 30 minutes. After the 30 minutes, the meat is turned over and fried for another 40 minutes. Now a crispy rind is created. Finally, pass the root vegetable sauce through a sieve and assemble with a little cold butter. Serve with the meat and enjoy.

Delicious pork medallions on toasted protein bread

454.8 kcal | 34.9 grams of protein | 31.8 grams of fat | 5.9 grams of carbohydrates **Ingredients:** 130 grams of pork loin, 2 mandarins, 1 chilli pepper, 1 spring onion, 80 grams of blue cheese, Himalayan salt, pepper, 1 tablespoon of butter, 1 clove of garlic, 2 slices of protein bread **Preparation:** Brush the bread with the butter and sprinkle on top it with the finely chopped garlic. Then roast it in the pan. Set the bread aside and cut the meat into 2 slices. Season it with salt and pepper and fry it with a little oil. Now put the meat on top of the bread. Now fillet the mandarins and toss it briefly in the pan with the finely chopped chilli pepper and the spring onion cut into rings. Season with salt and spread over the meat. Now spread the blue cheese on the bread and let it melt in the oven for 5 minutes.

Pork schnitzel with spinach and a delicious cream cheese coating

436.1 kcal | 37.6 grams of protein | 29.1 grams of fat | 3.4 grams of carbohydrates **Ingredients:** 160 grams of pork schnitzel, 50 grams of mascarpone, 1 shallot, juice of half an organic lemon, 50 grams of spinach leaves, 1 clove of garlic, Himalayan salt, pepper, 1 pinch of ground cardamom, 50 ml of broth, 1 teaspoon of butter **Preparation:** Pound the meat thinly and cut the shallot and garlic into small pieces and sauté in the pan. Chop the spinach coarsely and add it to the pan as well. Now stir it with the mascarpone, but do not bring to the boil. Spread the mixture over half of the schnitzel, fold it shut, and fix with a toothpick. Then season with salt and pepper and fry on both sides in the pan. Now add the broth and close it with a lid, simmer for about 10 minutes on a low level. Finally refine with cardamom and butter and serve with the sauce. They will love it ??

Delicious game dishes

Schnitzel (deer) with a difference with Romanesco florets

221.6 kcal | 24.2 grams of protein | 11 grams of fat | 4.5 grams of carbohydrates **Ingredients:** 140 grams of venison (loin), 1 clove of garlic, oil for frying, oregano, thyme, Himalayan salt, pepper, 100 ml of game stock or broth, 1 teaspoon of cold butter, 80 grams of romanesco, 2 cherry tomatoes

Preparation:

Cut the meat into 2 cm thick medallions and pound it thinly under cling film. Sprinkle it with salt and horses, and then fry it in oil with the whole clove of garlic and herbs. Take the meat out of the pan for a moment and pour in the stock, so that the frying residues dissolve. Stir in the cold butter with the whisk, but do not let it boil again. Now put the cherry tomatoes and medallions back in the pan and let it steep. Finally, only cook the Romanesco roses in salt water. Now you take it out and arrange it together with the medallions.

Yummy venison strips with crunchy red cabbage

Ingredients: 130 grams of venison fillet, 1 shallot, 60 grams of porcini mushrooms, rosemary, 1 clove of garlic, 1 tablespoon of sour cream, 150 ml of stock, thyme, marjoram, 1 splash of red wine vinegar, 1 tablespoon of cranberries (fresh or xylitol jam), 100 grams of red cabbage, 1 / 2 apples, 1/2 onions, 1 pinch of gingerbread spices, 100 ml naturally cloudy apple juice, Himalayan salt, pepper, some oil for frying **Preparation:** Cut the meat into small pieces and fry it in a little oil. Season it with salt and pepper and then remove it from the pan. Cut the shallots and garlic into fine pieces and sweat them in the pan you just used. Now cut the porcini mushrooms and add them to the pan with the herbs. Then it is extinguished with the red wine vinegar. Add the stock and put the meat back in the pan. Now bind the sauce with the sour cream and stir in the cranberries. Now cut half the onion into small pieces and sweat it in a little oil. Slice the apple into fine pieces and add it. Then the red cabbage is cut into fine strips and also placed in the pan. Season with salt, pepper, the gingerbread spice and a dash of vinegar. Finally pour the apple juice over it and let it simmer for about 20 minutes with the lid on over low heat. Serve and enjoy.

Venison schnitzel, baked with pumpkin seed breading and salad

592.1 kcal | 49 grams of protein | 38.6 grams of fat | 11.8 grams of carbohydrates **Ingredients:** 140 grams of beef loin, 10 grams of almond flour, 1 egg, 60 grams of chopped pumpkin seeds, Himalayan salt, pepper, oil for baking, 100 grams of lamb's lettuce, 1 shallot, 2 tablespoons of vinegar, 1 dash of sweetener, 1 tablespoon of oil, 3 tbsp water **Preparation:** First cut the meat into slices and pound it thinly, then season with salt and pepper. Roll the meat in the almond flour and then pull it through the beaten egg and coat it with the pumpkin seeds. Now bake the meat in hot oil and then let it drain well on a paper towel. Wash the lamb's lettuce and chop the shallot into very fine pieces. To make the marinade, mix the vinegar, oil, water, sweetener, salt and pepper together well. Now pour the marinade over the salad and serve it with the pumpkin seed schnitzel.

WILD STEAK SANDWICH

Who says the roast beef can only be eaten as a dish? Also in the morning for breakfast it is an enrichment for our senses. Of course, you can also serve it on a delicious salad.

For real meat lovers: roast beef

1934 kcal | 323 grams of protein | 63.4 grams of fat | 1.1 grams of carbohydrates **Ingredients:** 2 kg of deer loin, 1 tablespoon of mustard, salt, coarse pepper, rosemary, 1 bulb of garlic, thyme, Himalayan salt, marjoram **Preparation:** Brush the meat with mustard, salt and pepper. Now put together with the meat, rosemary, marjoram, thyme and garlic in a pan and sauté it. Then the pan is placed in the oven at 120 ° Celsius for 60 minutes. Then take the meat out and let it steep a little. Cut it into thin slices and enjoy. ??

Fresh steak sandwich

249.4 kcal | 24.3 grams of protein | 10.7 grams of fat | 8.3 grams of carbohydrates **Ingredients:** 2 slices of protein bread, 2 teaspoons of cream cheese, 2 leaves of iceberg lettuce, 1/2 tomato, 2 slices of roast beef, a few slices of cucumber, 1/2 teaspoon of freshly grated horseradish **Preparation:** Spread the cream cheese on the bread and top it with the lettuce, tomatoes and cucumbers. Scatter the horseradish on top, place the roast beef on top and close.

BEEF DISHES

Viennese-style soup pot with boiled beef

185 kcal | 25.5 grams of protein | 7.7 grams of fat | 3 grams of carbohydrates **Ingredients:** 100 grams of boiled beef, 1/2 carrot, 30 grams of celery, 1 bay leaf, 10 grams of parsley roots, Himalayan salt, peppercorns, 2 juniper berries, 250 ml of vegetable broth, 30 grams of konjac noodles **Preparation:** Cut the meat and vegetables into small pieces and cook it together with the spices in the broth. After about an hour, the meat should be heavenly tender. Fish out the bay leaf and grains and then add the konjac noodles to the soup.

Juicy fillet of beef in a delicious cassis sauce

371.7 kcal | 41.4 grams of protein | 7.3 grams of fat | 32 grams of carbohydrates **Ingredients:** 180 grams of beef fillet, 1 shallot, 1 clove of garlic, 1/2 teaspoon of lavender, 10 grams of carrots, 10 grams of celery, 50 ml of cassis juice, 50 ml of broth, 2 tablespoons of balsamic vinegar, 2 tablespoons of olive oil for frying, Himalayan salt, pepper **Preparation:** Fry the fillet on all sides in olive oil, then take it out of the pan and let it simmer in the oven for 20 minutes at 100 ° Celsius. Now put the sliced shallots, the chopped garlic, carrot and celery in the pan you used previously. Deglaze the whole thing with balsamic vinegar and add the lavender. Now pour in the broth and juice and let it reduce. Season to taste with salt and pepper, then puree the sauce and serve with the fillet.

Sweet and spicy: Beiriedschnitte in chocolate-chilli sauce

345.8 kcal | 37.2 grams of protein | 17 grams of fat | 8.4 grams of carbohydrates **Ingredients:** 150 grams of beetroot, 1 shallot, 1 clove of garlic, 1/2 chilli pepper, 15 grams of grated xylitol, dark chocolate, thyme, rosemary, Himalayan salt, pepper, 20 ml of cream, 70 ml of stock **Preparation:** Season that Beiried with salt and pepper and then fry it together with the herbs in a pan. Take the meat out of the pan and let it cook in the oven at around 50 ° Celsius. Cut the onion and garlic into small pieces and sweat them with the chilli. Then pour in the stock and melt the chocolate in it. Add the cream and season with salt and horses. Briefly add the meat and serve.

Juicy fillet of beef served with fresh prawns

242.4 kcal | 41.2 grams of protein | 6.2 grams of fat | 4.7 grams of

carbohydrates **Ingredients:** 150 grams of beef fillet, 100 grams of king prawns, Himalayan salt, steak pepper, 3 cloves of garlic, thyme, 2 tablespoons of olive oil **Preparation:** To start, fry the beef fillet on both sides in a pan. Now take the beef fillet out of the pan and bake it in the oven at 120 ° Celsius for 15 minutes. Next, chop the garlic and fry it together with the herbs and prawns until translucent. Now the beef fillet can be taken out of the oven, decorated with the prawns and poured over the garlic oil.

Delicious hip steak with red onion confit

Ingredients: 180 grams of hip steak, 2 red onions, 1 clove of garlic, 1/2 vanilla pod, marjoram, thyme, Himalayan salt, pepper, 100 ml stock, zest of an organic lime, 1 tbsp butter

Preparation:
To begin with, the hip steak is cut into seared in a grill pan without oil. Grill each side for about 3 to 4 minutes. First of all, the onions must be halved and cut into strips. Now chop the garlic finely and sweat it with the onions in butter until it is nice and translucent. Now add the

pulp of the vanilla pod and season the whole thing with salt and pepper. Now pour in the broth and let it simmer. Serve the red onion confit with the steak.

FRESH FISH DISHES

Grilled pears with fresh catfish

382 kcal | 25.4 grams of protein | 24.1 grams of fat | 14.5 grams of carbohydrates **Ingredients:** 160 grams of catfish fillet, 1 pear, 1 teaspoon of dill, Himalayan salt, pepper, 2 cloves of garlic, juice of an organic lemon, 1 tablespoon of butter, 2 tablespoons of olive oil **Preparation:** Salt and pepper the fish and sprinkle with it the lemon juice. Then fry it in olive oil. First of all, the pear needs to be cut into wedges. Then fry them in butter. Add the finely chopped garlic to the pear. Now refine the whole thing with dill and a little lemon juice. Season with salt and pepper if necessary. Serve the grilled pears with the fried fish.

Potato flakes on a juicy trout fillet

278 kcal | 23.7 grams of protein | 13.7 grams of fat | 13.8 grams of

carbohydrates **Ingredients:** 160 grams of trout fillet, Himalayan salt, pepper, juice of an organic lemon, 1 potato, 2 tablespoons of olive oil, 1 clove of garlic, 1/4 bunch of basil **Preparation:** At the beginning the fish is salted, peppered and soured. Peel the potatoes and grate them into fine slices. Line the skin side of the fish with the potatoes so that they look like scales. Press the potato well. The egg white and potato starch ensure that these stick very well to the fish. Finally add a little salt. Now fry the fish in oil with the potato side down. After 4 minutes, this can be carefully turned over with a spatula. Let the fish cook for another 3 minutes. Chop the garlic and mix it with the basil and 1 tablespoon olive oil in a mortar. After serving the fish, the marinade can be drizzled over the fish. This gives the whole thing a special aroma.

Tasty squid soup

78 kcal | 13 grams of protein | 1.1 grams of fat | 3.3 grams of carbohydrates **Ingredients:** 120 grams of baby squids cleaned, Himalayan salt, pepper, 1 chilli pepper, stick of ginger the size of a thumbnail, 1/2 stick of celery, 1/4 bunch of coriander, 1 shallot, 200

ml of broth, 1 teaspoon of oil **Preparation:** To start sweat the garlic, chilli, and ginger in a very little oil. Add the chopped squid and roast it briefly. Take everything out of the pan and pour in the broth. Chop the celery and add it to the soup. Then coarsely chop the coriander and add it back to the soup together with the squid mixture. Let this simmer for a few minutes and season to taste with salt, pepper and possibly fish sauce.

Delicious sesame cucumber salad with tuna

278.5 kcal | 40.1 grams of protein | 10.7 grams of fat | 6 grams of carbohydrates **Ingredients:** 150 grams of tuna steak, juice of an organic lime, 10 grams of sesame seeds, 1/2 cucumber, 1 tablespoon sesame oil, 1 tablespoon rice wine vinegar, 1 dash of soy sauce, Himalayan salt, pepper, 1 tablespoon of chopped coriander **Preparation:** Fry the tuna steak in a grill pan with fat. Then salt, pepper and sour it. Make sure that it does not get too dry, but that it is still glassy on the inside. Toast the sesame seeds without fat in the pan and cut the cucumber into 1 cm cubes. Marinate these with vinegar and sesame oil. Then the whole thing is seasoned with soy sauce. Now add the sesame seeds and fold in the finely chopped coriander. Serve the juicy tuna steak with the sesame cucumber salad.

Fresh baby spinach on seafood

227.2 kcal | 25.2 grams of protein | 10 grams of fat | 7.4 grams of carbohydrates **Ingredients:** 150 grams of seafood mixed, fresh or frozen, 1 shallot, 1 clove of garlic, juice of an organic lemon, 1 tablespoon of cashew nuts, 1 teaspoon of dill finely chopped, 100 grams of baby spinach, Himalayan salt, pepper **Preparation:** To At the beginning, the spinach is briefly blanched in salted water. First, the shallot and garlic are finely chopped and sweated in a little oil. First add the seafood and fry them, stirring constantly. Now the cashew nuts and the spinach have to be fried in the pan. Season this to taste with salt, pepper and lemon juice. To give you a fresh taste, sprinkle the dish with a little dill.

FAST MAIN COURSES

The pollack gourmet fillet in a class of its own

319.1 kcal | Protein: 29.9 grams | Fat: 20.3 grams | Carbohydrates: 4.2 grams **Preparation time:** 25 minutes **Ingredients:** 140 grams of pollack fillet | Himalayan salt | white pepper | Lemon juice | 1 tbsp butter | 1 teaspoon dill chopped | 1 teaspoon chives in rolls | 2 tbsp grated almonds | 1 pinch of medium-hot mustard with no added sugar **Preparation:** Salt and pepper the fish and drizzle with lemon juice. Now knead the butter with the dill, the chives, the almonds and the mustard and spread on the fish. The whole thing can be put in a small baking dish and the oven heated to 180 ° Celsius. Let the fish cook on top and bottom heat for 15 minutes. After the cooking time, enjoy the fish with a small mixed salad.

Healthy zucchini spaghetti with fresh prawns

159.7 kcal | Protein: 21.8 grams | Fat: 5.7 grams | Carbohydrates: 5.3 grams **Preparation time:** 12 minutes **Ingredients:** 1 zucchini | 1/2 red onion | 2 cloves of garlic | 1 tbsp butter | 100 grams of shrimp without shell | 1/2 red pepper | Juice of half a lemon | Himalayan salt | Pepper | 1/2 tbsp coriander chopped | 1/2 teaspoon rosemary finely chopped **Preparation:** Use a vegetable peeler to turn the zucchini into fine noodles. First, chop the onion and garlic and cut the peppers into strips. Now the butter can be heated in a pan and the prawns fried with onion, garlic and paprika for 2 minutes. Then add the zucchini noodles and toss the whole thing through the rosemary and coriander. First deglaze everything with the lemon juice and season with salt and pepper. Let the dish simmer for about 2 minutes over medium heat. Finally, it can be served and consumed.

Low carb burger alla Roma (Italian style)

297.5 kcal | Protein: 36 grams | Fat: 15.1 grams | Carbohydrates: 4.4 grams **Preparation time:** 15 minutes **Ingredients:** 150 grams of ground beef | 1/2 onion | 1 clove of garlic | 1/2 teaspoon hot mustard with no added sugar | rubbed some thyme | 1 pinch of ground caraway seeds | 1 tomato | 1/2 scoop of mozzarella | 8 basil leaves | Salt and pepper **Preparation:** Finely chop the onion and garlic and knead everything with the meat and mustard. Now season a little with salt and pepper and season with thyme and caraway seeds. Shape the mixture into two patties with wet hands and fry them in a non-oiled pan on all sides for 2 minutes. Use the patties as "burger bread". First cut the tomato and mozzarella into slices and layer them together with the basil between the meat loaves. Place the meat patties on a baking sheet lined with baking paper and bake them in the oven at 200 ° for 3 minutes.

Grandma's Secret Szeged Chicken Goulash

331.8 kcal | Protein: 38.9 grams | Fat: 17.8 grams | Carbohydrates: 4 grams **Preparation time:** 25 minutes **Ingredients:** 120 grams of chicken thighs raised | 1/2 onion | 1 clove of garlic | 1 teaspoon tomato paste with no added sugar | 1/2 teaspoon mild paprika | 1 pinch of hot pepper | Dried thyme | Dried marjoram | Cumin | 150 ml chicken broth | 50 grams of sauerkraut with no added sugar | Salt | Pepper | 1 tbsp vegetable oil | 1 tbsp creme fraiche **Preparation:** At the beginning cut the chicken into 1 cm cubes. Then chop the onion and garlic and fry everything in vegetable oil for 3 minutes. Add the tomato paste and roast it for 2 minutes. First, paprika, thyme and marjoram can be added and roasted briefly. Pour the chicken broth over the top and let it simmer for 12 minutes. Now add the sauerkraut and season with salt, pepper and cumin. When everything has simmered for 5 minutes over medium heat, the Szegedin chicken goulash can be arranged and garnished with the crème fraîche before serving.

Delicious tomato and spring onion salad with monkfish skewer

216.2 kcal | Protein: 25.3 grams | Fat: 11.8 grams | Carbohydrates: 2.2 grams **Preparation time:** 12 minutes **Ingredients** : 150 grams of monkfish fillet | 2 slices of bacon | Himalayan salt | Steak pepper | some lime juice | 1 stick of lemongrass | 3 spring onions with green | 40 grams of cherry tomatoes yellow | 40 cherry tomatoes red | 1/2 bunch of chervil chopped | 1 tbsp apple cider vinegar | 1 tbsp olive oil | 1 dash of sweetener **Preparation:** Salt and pepper the fish and then acidify it with lime juice. Now cut into 3 equal pieces. Skewer the pieces alternately with the bacon on the lemongrass. Now the whole thing can be seared in a grill pan without fat on all sides for 4 minutes each. Cut the spring onion into rings, cut the cherry tomatoes in half and mix everything with the chervil. Marinate the whole thing with a dressing of apple cider vinegar, olive oil and sweetener and serve this with the skewer. The lemongrass gives the dish an extra flavor.

Delicious turkey schnitzel filled with cheese, onion and chili

280 kcal | Protein: 40.7 grams | Fat: 12 grams | Carbohydrates: 2.3 grams

Preparation time: 17 minutes **Ingredients:** 140 grams of turkey schnitzel | Salt and pepper | 20 grams of grated Emmental cheese | 1/2 red onion | 1 red chilli | 2 sage leaves | 1 tablespoon of grated mountain cheese **Preparation:** Beat the turkey thinly and season the meat with salt and pepper. Now cut the onion and chilli into slices and mix with the chopped sage and grated Emmentaler. Spread the whole thing over the schnitzel and fold the meat in. Finally fix it with a toothpick. Place the turkey schnitzel on a baking sheet lined with baking paper and sprinkle with the mountain cheese. Heat the oven to 170 ° Celsius and let the turkey cook on top and bottom heat for 12 minutes.

Fried watermelon with beef tenderloin

319.3 kcal | Protein: 34.8 grams | Fat: 16.5 grams | Carbohydrates: 7.9 grams

Preparation time : 10 minutes **Ingredients:** 180 grams of beef fillet

| Fleur de Sel | colored pepper | 1 sprig of rosemary | 2 sprigs of thyme | 2 cloves of garlic | 1 tbsp olive oil | 100 grams of watermelon seedless

Preparation:

Salt and pepper the meat and fry it in olive oil along with rosemary, thyme and garlic. The meat is seared on each side for about 3 minutes. As soon as you turn the meat, you can also add the watermelon to the pan. Now everything can be arranged together and, if necessary, a little salt and pepper.

Rocket on prawns with black sesame seeds

350.9 kcal | Protein: 31.7 grams | Fat: 21.3 grams | Carbohydrates: 8.1 grams **Preparation time:** 11 minutes **Ingredients:** 140 grams of shrimp without shell and cleaned | 1 tbsp sesame oil | 1 tbsp black sesame seeds | Juice and zest of an untreated organic lime | Himalayan salt | Pepper | 50 grams of arugula | 1 tbsp roasted pine nuts | 1/4 yellow pepper | 2 date tomatoes | 1 teaspoon raspberry vinegar | 2 tbsp water | 1 tbsp walnut oil | 40 grams of fresh or frozen raspberries **Preparation** : Fry the prawns in sesame oil for 2 minutes until translucent and then sprinkle them with the sesame. Season the prawns with salt, pepper, lime juice and zest. Now the raspberry vinegar can be mixed with water and walnut oil and gently seasoned with salt and pepper. Cut peppers into cubes and tomatoes into slices. Mix both with the rocket and fold in the pine nuts and raspberries first. Now marinate with the dressing and serve with the prawns. A slice of toasted protein bread can be served to match.

Delicious almond spinach with pikeperch

365 kcal | Protein: 32.5 grams | Fat: 22.6 grams | Carbohydrates: 7.9 grams

Preparation time: 12 minutes

Ingredients: 150 grams of pikeperch fillet | 80 grams of spinach leaves | 1/2 onion | 1 clove of garlic | 1 pinch of baking soda | 2 tbsp almonds chopped | 60 ml cream | Salt and pepper | ground some nutmeg | some lemon juice | 2 teaspoons of butter

Preparation:
Salt and pepper the fish and acidify it with the lemon juice. Fry it skin

side down in a teaspoon of butter. Fry on the skin side for 3 minutes, then remove from the heat, turn and let steep for 2 minutes. Cut the onion and garlic into small pieces and sweat everything together with the chopped almonds in the remaining butter until translucent. Roughly chop the spinach leaves and add them. Pour the cream on top and add baking soda. Now the whole thing is seasoned with salt, pepper and nutmeg. Let the almond spinach simmer for a minute and serve it with the pikeperch.

Chicken schnitzel wrapped in a parmesan egg shell

459.4 kcal | Protein: 58.3 grams | Fat: 24.6 grams | Carbohydrates: 1.2 grams

Preparation time: 10 minutes

Ingredients: 140 grams of chicken schnitzel | Salt and pepper | 2 sage leaves | 1 tbsp almond flour | 1 egg | 3 teaspoons of parmesan, finely grated | 1 teaspoon vegetable oil | 1 teaspoon butter

Preparation:
Knock the schnitzel thinly and season with salt and then pepper. Now press the sage well onto the meat. First roll the meat in flour. Whisk the egg and mix it with the parmesan. Pull the schnitzel through the

egg. Now heat the vegetable oil together with the butter in a pan and fry the schnitzel in it until golden brown.

Delicious pork fillet with paprika gorgonzola sauce

232.4 kcal | Protein: 37.6 grams | Fat: 7.6 grams | Carbohydrates: 3.4 grams **Preparation time** : 12 minutes **Ingredients:** 150 grams of pork tenderloin | 1 tbsp olive oil | 1 shallot | 1/2 red pepper | 1/2 teaspoon sweet paprika | 1 tbsp apple cider vinegar | 1 pinch of ginger powder | 80 ml of broth | 10 grams of Gorgonzola or blue cheese of your choice | 1 tbsp chives in rolls | Salt and pepper **Preparation:** Divide the pork tenderloin into three medallions of the same size and flatten them lightly with your hand. Then salt and pepper the meat and brush with the paprika powder. Cut the shallot and bell pepper into strips. Fry the meat in olive oil on both sides for 2 minutes each, take it out of the pan and keep it warm. Roast the shallot and bell pepper in the same pan and deglaze with apple cider vinegar. Season the whole thing with ginger and pour the broth over everything. Bring this to the boil briefly and then crumble the Gorgonzola. Let the cheese melt over medium heat, stirring constantly. First put the meat back in the pan, toss briefly and serve. Finally, sprinkle the dish with chives or herbs of your choice.

The original minced meat pan with basil from Asia

333.4 kcal | Protein: 44.2 grams | Fat: 14.6 grams | Carbohydrates: 6.3 grams **Preparation time:** 18 minutes **Ingredients:** 130 grams of minced poultry | 1/2 onion | 1/2 teaspoon curry paste red from the Asia store | Juice of half a lime | 1/2 stick of celery | 50 ml coconut milk | 1 pinch of xylitol or a splash of sweetener | Soy sauce | Fish sauce | 8 basil leaves | 1 dried chilli pepper | 2 tbsp hazelnuts chopped | 50 ml broth | 1 teaspoon coconut oil **Preparation:** At the beginning, dice the onion and fry it together with the minced meat in coconut oil. Add the curry paste and roast it for a few minutes. Chop the celery and put it in the pan. Now season with lime juice, soy sauce and fish sauce. Add the whole dried chilli and the hazelnuts. Then season the whole thing with sweetener. Delete everything with the broth and pour the coconut milk on it. Finally, let it simmer for 5 minutes over a medium heat, season as required and serve.

Broccoli and cauliflower with delicious salmon

460.7 kcal | Protein: 32.4 grams | Fat: 32.7 grams | Carbohydrates: 9.2 grams **Preparation time:** 15 minutes **Ingredients:** 130 grams of skinless salmon fillet | 50 grams of broccoli | 50 grams of cauliflower | 100 ml cream | 2 tbsp cream cheese | 1 tbsp lovage chopped (Maggi herb) | Juice of half a lemon | Salt and pepper | 1 tbsp roasted almond flakes **Preparation:** Salt and pepper the fish and place it in a small baking dish. First, cut the broccoli and cauliflower into small florets and drape them around the fish. Mix the cream cheese with lovage and lemon juice and season with salt and pepper. Spread everything over the fish and sprinkle with flaked almonds. Preheat the oven to 180 ° Celsius and cook the fish in a fan oven for 12 minutes.

Delicious pumpkin crust on pork loin steak

452.5 kcal | Protein: 44.3 grams | Fat: 25.7 grams | Carbohydrates: 11 grams

Preparation time: 18 minutes **Ingredients:** 160 grams of pork loin steak without rind | Salt and pepper | 50 grams of pumpkin | 1 tbsp chopped pumpkin seeds | 1 egg yolk | some dried marjoram | 2 tbsp oat bran | 1/2 teaspoon freshly torn horseradish **Preparation:** Salt and pepper the meat at the beginning and fry it in a grill pan without fat on both sides for 2 minutes each. First grate the pumpkin finely and mix it with the chopped pumpkin seeds, egg yolk, marjoram, oat bran and horseradish. Season the whole thing with salt and pepper. Cover the meat with the mass and place it on a baking sheet lined with parchment paper. Preheat the oven to 170 ° Celsius and bake the meat for 12 minutes on top and bottom heat.

Delicious chicken in a delicious mushroom sauce

238.8 kcal | Protein: 42 grams | Fat: 6.4 grams | Carbohydrates: 3.3 grams

Preparation time: 15 minutes **Ingredients:** 120 grams of skinless chicken breast | 4 mushrooms | 3 small shallots | 1/4 yellow carrot | 120 ml chicken broth | 2 tbsp sour cream | some thyme fresh or dried | 1 teaspoon parsley chopped | Salt and pepper | 1 dash of lemon juice **Preparation:** Cut the chicken into thin strips and quarter the mushrooms. Also cut the carrot into small cubes. Now bring the broth to the boil and add the meat, the mushrooms, the sliced shallots and the diced carrot. Let the whole boil for 10 minutes and then stir in the sour cream. Season everything with thyme and then season with salt, pepper and lemon juice. Let simmer for another 2 minutes over medium heat and sprinkle with parsley before serving.

Tender veal schnitzel gratinated with delicious sheep cheese and delicious bacon

558 kcal | Protein: 39.9 grams | Fat: 43.6 grams | Carbohydrates: 1.6 grams **Preparation time:** 14 minutes **Ingredients:** 140 grams of veal schnitzel | 1 tbsp almond flour | Salt and pepper | 1 tbsp butter | 1 tbsp bacon diced | 30 grams goat cheese soft | 1 teaspoon walnuts chopped | 1 tbsp parsley chopped | 60 ml vegetable broth **Preparation:** At the beginning the schnitzel is pounded thinly and then salted and peppered. Fry the schnitzel in butter on both sides for one minute each. Take it out of the pan and stir the almond flour into the remaining butter. Now the whole thing can be infused with the broth. Stir everything with the whisk, bring it to a boil and then set it aside. First place the schnitzel on a baking tray lined with

baking paper and mix the bacon cubes with goat cheese, walnuts and parsley. Spread the mixture over the meat and let everything bake at 180 ° Celsius and top and bottom heat for 8 minutes. Finally, the schnitzel can be arranged on a plate and poured over with the sauce.

Venison fillet on delicious pumpkin

366.7 kcal | Protein: 33.4 grams | Fat: 24.7 grams | Carbohydrates: 2.7 grams **Preparation time:** 18 minutes **Ingredients:** 140 grams of venison fillet | Salt and pepper | 1 tbsp olive oil | 1/2 teaspoon parsley chopped | 1/2 teaspoon chervil chopped | 1/2 teaspoon rosemary finely chopped | 1 teaspoon hazelnuts chopped | 80 grams of Hokkaido pumpkin | some thyme | 1 pinch of paprika powder mild | 1 pinch of cinnamon **Preparation:** Salt and pepper the meat and fry it in olive oil on all sides for about 3 minutes. Now mix the parsley, chervil, rosemary and hazelnuts and roll the meat in them. Now press the breading well with your hands and place the meat on a baking tray lined with baking paper. Cut the pumpkin into slices about 0.5 cm thick and season them with thyme, paprika, cinnamon, salt and pepper. Now place these on the baking sheet and bake everything together at 160 ° Celsius, with top and bottom heat, for 15 minutes.

Delicious minced meat pan with fresh mushrooms

355.5 kcal | Protein: 30.1 grams | Fat: 21.9 grams | Carbohydrates: 9.5 grams **Preparation time:** 14 minutes **Ingredients:** 130 grams of minced beef, lean | 1/2 onion | 50 grams of chanterelles | 50 grams of king oyster mushrooms | 1/4 pear | 2 tbsp apple cider vinegar | 100 ml vegetable stock | 50 ml cream | Salt and pepper | dried marjoram | 1 tbsp chives in rolls | 1 teaspoon olive oil **Preparation:** At the beginning, cut the onion into small pieces and fry it together with the minced meat in olive oil. First, the chanterelles and mushrooms can be cut into bite-sized pieces and also placed in the pan. Now dice the pear, add it and toss it through the pan. Then deglaze the whole thing with apple cider vinegar. Now add the broth and season with salt, pepper and marjoram. Let everything simmer for about 8 minutes. Finally, add the cream to the dish. Let this simmer briefly, arrange and sprinkle with chives before serving.

VEGATARIAN LUNCH

Tofu with delicious vegetarian red Thai curry

586.1 kcal | 28.1 grams of protein | 44.3 grams of fat | 6.9 grams of carbohydrates **Ingredients:** 150 grams of firm tofu, 1 teaspoon of red curry paste from the Asia Shop, 200 ml of coconut milk, 4 cocktail tomatoes, 4 lychee, (fresh or canned, make sure that these are not sugared), 1 lime leaf, Fish sauce, soy sauce, sweetener, 1 teaspoon basil leaves **Preparation:** Toast the curry paste in a pan without fat. Now pour the coconut milk on it and stir it well. Now add the lime leaf and the cut tofu. After the whole thing has simmered for a minute, add the quartered lychee and the halved cocktail tomatoes. Season the curry with soy sauce, fish sauce and a splash of liquid sweetener. Before the dish is served, sprinkle the basil leaves over it. Do you prefer something hotter? Then add a few more chilli flakes.

Delicious konjac noodles with crunchy vegetables

251.9 kcal | 21.6 grams of protein | 14.4 grams of fat | 6.5 grams of carbohydrates **Ingredients:** 100 grams of smoked tofu, 100 grams of konjac noodles, 2 cherry tomatoes, 1/2 yellow bell pepper, 1/2 stick of celery, 1 teaspoon parsley, 1 teaspoon coriander, 2 tbsp soy sauce, 1 chilli pepper, 1 tbsp Low carb ketchup, 1 tbsp peanuts coarsely chopped, 2 tbsp nut oil, juice of half an organic lime, 1 spring onion for garnish **Preparation:** Soak the konjac noodles briefly in hot water. Dice all the ingredients and fry them in oil. A wok pan is perfect for this. Delete the vegetables with the lime juice and stir in the ketchup. Now the pasta can be mixed in and the herbs added. Season the whole thing with soy sauce. Garnish the dish with the finely chopped spring onion before serving.

Fresh cauliflower baked with cheese

485.6 kcal | 39 grams of protein | 32.6 grams of fat | 7.1 grams of carbohydrates **Ingredients:** 150 grams of cauliflower, 1 tablespoon of butter, 1/2 onion, 1 clove of garlic, 50 ml of cream, 50 grams of Gouda cheese, 50 grams of Parmesan, Himalayan salt, pepper, 2 tablespoons of cream cheese, marjoram, 1 tablespoon of chopped pine nuts **Preparation:** Let the cauliflower cook in salted water until al dente. Sweat the finely chopped onion and garlic in butter. Now the pine nuts are also roasted and poured with cream. Add salt, pepper and marjoram to taste, stir in the cream cheese and add the parmesan. Cut the cauliflower into bite-sized pieces and add these to the pan as well. Now pour everything into an ovenproof dish and sprinkle with Gouda cheese. This is baked at 160 ° Celsius for about 12 minutes.

Cabbage rolls filled with delicious goat cheese

683.4 kcal | 45.2 grams of protein | 54.2 grams of fat | 4.2 grams of carbohydrates **Ingredients:** 150 grams of goat cheese / feta, 4 large cabbage leaves, 1 teaspoon parsley, 1/2 teaspoon dill, Himalayan salt, pepper, 1 pinch of caraway seeds, 1 egg, 1 tablespoon of olive oil **Preparation:** Blanch the cabbage leaves in Salt water. The hard stalk must be removed beforehand. Knead the crumbled goat cheese with the herbs and egg. Now season with caraway seeds, salt and pepper. Now place the feta mass on the cabbage leaves and wrap them in small roulades. Fix the roulades with a toothpick. Now fry all sides in olive oil and then place the pan in the oven for 15 minutes at 150 ° Celsius. A piece of protein bread can be eaten with the cabbage rolls.

Two kinds of asparagus in a fruity, spicy tomato sauce

112.7 kcal | 4.6 grams of protein | 5.5 grams of fat | 9.6 grams of carbohydrates It doesn't always have to be hollandaise sauce. If you prepare your asparagus with this low carb sauce, you will save a lot of calories and fat. **Ingredients:** 100 grams of white asparagus, 100 grams of green asparagus, 1/2 can of pizza tomatoes, 1 shallot, 1 clove of garlic, oregano, 1 chilli pepper, Himalayan salt, pepper, 4 strawberries, basil, 1 tablespoon of olive oil, juice of an organic lemon **Preparation:** Cooking Put the asparagus in water with salt and lemon juice and then keep it warm. Lightly sweat the finely chopped shallots and garlic. Add the pizza tomatoes and refine it with the chilli, oregano and marjoram. Now season with salt and pepper and simmer for 5 minutes. Dice the strawberries, chop the basil and mix them with olive oil. Now serve the asparagus with the tomato sauce and cover it with the strawberries.

LUNCH SALAD

Fresh spinach leaves with grilled chicken liver

221.4 calories | 29.4 grams of protein | 6.5 grams of fat | 9.2 grams of carbohydrates **Ingredients:** 100 grams of poultry liver, 10 grams of diced breakfast bacon, 1 shallot, 200 grams of spinach leaves, 2 tablespoons of walnut oil, 2 tablespoons of white balsamic vinegar, 80 grams of sunflower sprouts, Himalayan salt, pepper, 1 tomato, 1 tablespoon of sour Cream **Preparation:** Fry the liver in very little oil with the chopped shallots and the diced bacon. Then briefly blanch the spinach leaves in salted water. Now mix vinegar, oil, salt and pepper to a marinade and marinate the spinach leaves with it. Now the sprouts have to be lifted up and arranged on a plate. Spread the liver on top and garnish with the sour cream. Finally, sprinkle everything with the finely diced tomato.

Spicy Thai Mango Salad

150.9 kcal | 3.9 grams of protein | 6.3 grams of fat | 17.8 grams of carbohydrates **Ingredients:** 1 green, sour mango, 1/2 carrot, 50 grams of white cabbage, 3 cocktail tomatoes, 1 small chilli pepper, 1 clove of garlic, 1 tablespoon of peanuts, juice of an organic lime, fish sauce, soy sauce, a dash of sweetener **Preparation:** cut Cut the cabbage, carrot and mango into long strips. This works best with a vegetable peeler or a vegetable grater. First, chop the chilli pepper and garlic. Then process this together with the lime juice, the fish sauce, the soy sauce and the sweetener to a marinade. Put it on the mango, carrot, cabbage and halved tomatoes and sprinkle with roughly chopped peanuts.

The combination makes it: asparagus and zucchini salad with fresh goat cheese

520.4 kcal | 27.8 grams of protein | 42.9 grams of fat | 3.6 grams of carbohydrates **Ingredients:** 150 grams of green asparagus, 1 yellow zucchini, 3 cherry tomatoes, 100 grams of grainy goat cream cheese, Himalayan salt, pepper, 3 tablespoons of olive oil, 2 tablespoons of white balsamic vinegar, 1/2 bunch of mint, 1 tablespoon of parsley, 2 spring onions **Preparation:** Cut the zucchini into thin strips with the peeler. Fry the zucchini and asparagus in olive oil. This is now extinguished with the vinegar and seasoned with salt and pepper. Let this cool down for a moment. Then fold in the grainy cream cheese, coarsely chopped mint, quartered tomatoes and parsley. Sprinkle the chopped green onions over the dish before serving.

Fresh apple and tuna salad

237.3 kcal | 26.7 grams of protein | 11.1 grams of fat | 6.5 grams of carbohydrates **Ingredients:** 1 can of tuna in its own juice, 1/2 apple, 50 grams of iceberg lettuce, 1 tomato, 1/4 cucumber, 1/2 yellow pepper, 1 tbsp finely chopped chives, 1 tbsp olive oil, 2 tbsp white wine vinegar, 1 hard-boiled egg, 1 small red onion **Preparation:** Cut all the ingredients into small pieces and then mix them together. Marinate the whole thing with the vinegar and the oil and then sprinkle everything with the chives.

Exotic mango and mushroom salad

Ingredients: 100 grams of lettuce, 1/4 carrot finely grated, 1/2 bunch of radishes, 100 grams of mushrooms, 2 tbsp chives, 1/2 mango, 2 tbsp yogurt, 1 tbsp olive oil, juice of an organic lime, pepper, 3 tbsp balsamic vinegar Dark vinegar, 1 tbsp chopped nuts **Preparation:** Mix the yoghurt, the olive oil and the lime juice to a marinade. Now put this marinade on the spinach leaves, radishes and carrots. Cut the mango and mushrooms into large cubes and fry them in very little olive oil. Then deglaze with the balsamic vinegar. Finally, arrange the mushrooms and mangoes on the salad and sprinkle with the nuts.

DINNER RECIPES

Creamy soup made from wild garlic

130.1 kcal | 3.3 grams of protein | 10 grams of fat | 6.2 grams of carbohydrates **Ingredients:** 60 grams of wild garlic (our tip: collect in spring and freeze in portions), 150 ml vegetable stock, 50 ml cream, Himalayan salt, pepper, some nutmeg, juice of half an organic lemon **Preparation:** Briefly blanch the wild garlic in salt water. This gives the soup a nice green color. Heat the broth and add the wild garlic. Now the whole thing can be pureed and seasoned with salt, pepper, nutmeg and lemon juice. Finally refine with cream.

Ginger and carrot soup with a hint of coconut

83.2 kcal | 1.6 grams of protein | 4.6 grams of fat | 7.2 grams of carbohydrates **Ingredients:** 30 grams of carrots, 5 grams of ginger, 2 tablespoons of coconut milk, 1 stick of lemongrass, 200 ml of broth, Himalayan salt, pepper, 1 shallot, 1 teaspoon of roasted desiccated coconut for sprinkling **Preparation:** Cut the shallots and sweat them this together with the carrots. Now lightly roast the ginger and add the broth. Then bring to the boil together with the lemongrass. Season the soup with salt and pepper. First boil the carrots until soft and then remove the lemongrass. Tie the soup with the coconut milk and then puree everything. Before serving, sprinkle the roasted coconut flakes over the ginger and carrot soup.

Fine creamy mushroom soup with bacon topping

190.3 kcal | 9.2 grams of protein | 14.7 grams of fat | 4.7 grams of carbohydrates **Ingredients:** 50 grams of mushrooms, 30 grams of oyster mushrooms, 1 shallot, 1 clove of garlic, 150 ml of broth, 50 ml of cream, Himalayan salt, pepper, 20 grams of diced breakfast bacon, 1 tablespoon of butter, 1 teaspoon of oil **Preparation:** Sweat the finely chopped shallots and garlic in oil. Chop the mushrooms and add them. Pour broth on top and season everything with salt and pepper. Now add the cream, fry the bacon in the butter and add finely plucked oyster mushrooms. Now place the topping, made of bacon and oyster mushrooms, on the soup.

Walnuts in cream parsnip soup

Ingredients: 60 grams of parsnip root (resembles a parsley root, is only slightly thicker), 1/2 onion, 200 ml of broth, Himalayan salt, pepper, thyme, pointed vinegar, 1 pinch of caraway seeds, 2 tablespoons of walnut oil, 1 tablespoon of chopped walnuts , 30 ml cream **Preparation:** Sweat the onion and the diced parsnip in walnut oil. Then deglaze with vinegar and add the broth. Now season this with salt, pepper, thyme and caraway seeds. Let the parsnips cook until soft. Tie the soup with the cream and then puree it. Now the walnuts have to be roasted in a coated pan and sprinkled over the soup before serving.

Delicious Indian pineapple curry soup

112.6 kcal | 1.8 grams of protein | 4.6 grams of fat | 14.2 grams of carbohydrates **Ingredients:** 30 grams of pineapple, 1 potato, 1 teaspoon of yellow curry powder, 30 ml of coconut milk, 1 chilli pepper, 1 shallot, 1 clove of garlic, 200 ml of broth, Himalayan salt, pepper, 1 teaspoon of oil, parsley for sprinkling **Preparation:** Chop the shallot and garlic. Now sweat this in oil. Pour the shallot and garlic with the broth and add the sliced potato. Now add the pineapple, chilli and curry powder. Season to taste with salt and pepper. Let the potatoes boil until soft. Refine the soup with the coconut milk and puree. If you like, the dish can be sprinkled with parsley.

SALADS AND EXPRESS MEALS

Smoked salmon on colorful lettuce

294.3 kcal | 24.6 grams of protein | 16.1 grams of fat | 11.3 grams of carbohydrates **Ingredients:** 100 grams of smoked salmon, 150 grams of mixed lettuce, 1/2 bunch of basil, 1 tomato, 1/4 grated carrot, 1/2 apple, 3 radishes, 1 tablespoon quark, 2 tablespoons of olive oil, 1 tablespoon Apple cider vinegar , 5 grams of grated horseradish, Himalayan salt, pepper **Preparation:** Mix the quark, olive oil, vinegar, horseradish, salt and pepper to a marinade. Mix the lettuce with the carrots, the sliced tomatoes, the radishes and the chopped apple to form a salad. This can now be arranged on a plate. Pour the marinade over the salad. Finally, drape the smoked salmon on the salad.

Asian red curry with chicken on a fresh salad

328.2 kcal | 35.3 grams of protein | 12 grams of fat | 13.6 grams of carbohydrates

Ingredients: 50 grams of white cabbage, 1/2 grated carrot, 1/2 zucchini finely grated, 1/2 pear diced, 3 tbsp yogurt, juice of an organic lime, 1 tbsp sesame oil, 1 tbsp rice wine vinegar, 100 Gram of chicken breast finely chopped, 1/2 teaspoon of red curry paste, 1 tablespoon of coconut milk

Preparation:

Finely chop the cabbage and mix it with the carrot, zucchini and pear. Now fry the chicken in a pan with a little oil and then add the curry paste. Finally add the coconut milk and let it reduce. Then take the pan off the stove. Mix together yogurt, lime juice, sesame oil and vinegar to form a marinade. Mix this with the salad. Arrange the salad and garnish with the chicken.

Fruity, spicy: the slightly different steak salad

353.9 kcal | 27.1 grams of protein | 19.1 grams of fat | 19 grams of carbohydrates **Ingredients:** 100 grams of beef fillet, 1 peach, 50 grams of strawberries, 100 grams of rocket, 50 grams of frisee salad, 1 tablespoon of pine nuts, 1/2 yellow pepper, Himalayan salt, pepper, 1 tablespoon of coriander, 1/2 chilli pepper, 1 Garlic clove, juice of 2 organic limes, 2 tablespoons of olive oil, 1 splash of sweetener **Preparation:** Process coriander, chili, garlic, lime juice, olive oil and sweetener in a blender to make a marinade. Fry the beef fillet cut into strips in a grill pan without oil. Add the pine nuts and season with salt and pepper. Cut the peaches and strawberries into large cubes and the peppers into fine cubes. Marinate everything with the dressing. Finally fold in the salads and serve together with the fillet strips.

Italian style avocado caprese salad

625.6 kcal | 39.8 grams of protein | 45.7 grams of fat | 14.3 grams of carbohydrates **Ingredients:** 120 grams of baby mozzarella, 80 grams of red cherry tomatoes, 80 grams of yellow cherry tomatoes, 1 bunch of basil, 1/2 avocado, 3 tablespoons of olive oil, 3 tablespoons of white balsamic vinegar, Himalayan salt, pepper, 2 slices of prosciutto **Preparation:** First pull apart the baby mozzarella, halve the tomatoes and dice the avocado. Chop the basil and cut the prosciutto into strips. Now mix everything together. The whole thing is marinated with a dressing made from olive oil, vinegar, salt and pepper.

Grilled turkey strips on romaine lettuce with carrot-ginger dressing

276 kcal | 32.3 grams of protein | 4 grams of fat | 27 grams of carbohydrates

Ingredients: 100 grams of turkey, 100 grams of romaine lettuce, 50 ml of carrot juice, 5 grams of ginger, 3 cherry tomatoes, 2 radishes, 50 grams of bean sprouts, 1/2 yellow pepper, Himalayan salt, pepper, 2 tablespoons of vegetable oil, 2 tablespoons of apple cider vinegar

Preparation:
Press the ginger through the garlic press. Mix this with the carrot juice, vinegar, oil, salt and pepper to a marinade. Cut the turkey into strips and fry them in a non-oiled pan until crispy. Now roughly pluck the romaine lettuce and mix with the halved cherry tomatoes, the bean sprouts and the diced paprika. Cut the radishes into slices and add them. Finally marinate the whole thing with the dressing and serve the turkey on top.

Salad with nutty camembert

482.3 kcal | 27.6 grams of protein | 37.8 grams of fat | 7.1 grams of carbohydrates

Ingredients: 1 camembert, 15 grams of chopped nuts of your choice, 100 grams of endive salad, 1/4 yellow bell pepper, 1/4 red bell pepper, 1/2 stick of celery, 2 tablespoons walnut oil, 2 tablespoons raspberry vinegar, Himalaya Salt, pepper, 3 tablespoons of water

Preparation:
Thinly cut the lid off the camembert and let the cheese melt in the oven at 180 ° Celsius with the chopped nuts for about 15 minutes. The vinegar, oil, water, salt and pepper make the marinade. Cut the bell pepper and celery into pieces and mix them with the sliced endive salad. Pour the marinade on top. Now the salad can be eaten with the camembert. A piece of protein bread can be served to go with it.

Delicious sauces on steak variations

178.5 kcal | 34.5 grams of protein | 4.5 grams of fat | 0 grams of carbohydrates (excluding dip) **Ingredients:** 50 grams of beef fillet, 50 grams of pork fillet, 50 grams of poultry, Himalayan salt, pepper and various low carb dip sauces. **Preparation: Are** you suddenly hungry and not in the mood to cook something elaborate? Then fry a nice piece of meat in a pan and serve it with various low carb sauces. This dish is very tasty and it doesn't need a lot of ingredients.

The vitamin-rich alternative to fresh vegetables: frozen vegetables

264.9 kcal | 5.2 grams of protein | 21 grams of fat | 10.7 grams of carbohydrates **Ingredients:** 200 grams of frozen vegetables of your choice, Himalayan salt, pepper, 2 tablespoons of broth or water, 50 grams of sour cream, 1 tablespoon of chopped herbs. **Preparation:** Heat the frozen vegetables in a pan together with the broth and season this with salt and pepper. Now refine the whole thing with sour cream and stir in the herbs. It is often forgotten that frozen vegetables contain more vitamins than you initially think. Are you not a cook? Then this is the recipe for you.

Chicken schnitzel pizza style

331.5 kcal | 50.2 grams of protein | 10.9 grams of fat | 3.6 grams of carbohydrates **Ingredients:** 130 grams of chicken breast, 50 grams of mushrooms, 1/2 can of pizza tomatoes, 1 shallot, oregano, 1/4 bunch of basil, Himalayan salt, pepper, 1 tablespoon of parmesan **Preparation:** Pound the chicken thinly and fry put it on both sides in a coated pan. First sweat the shallots. Add the cut mushrooms and season everything with salt, pepper and the herbs. Add the pizza tomatoes. Then stir in the parmesan. This is now spread over the chicken and voilà, the creative pizza variation is ready.

DELICIOUS EGG DISHES

Mexican style scrambled eggs

443.9 kcal | 19.2 grams of protein | 36.2 grams of fat | 6.6 grams of carbohydrates **Ingredients:** 2 eggs, 1 tablespoon milk, Himalayan salt, pepper, 1 teaspoon olive oil, 1/4 red pepper, 1/2 chilli pepper, 2 slices of bacon, 1 tablespoon of coriander, 1 slice of protein bread **Preparation:** Whisk the eggs , Milk, salt and pepper together. First, the bacon has to be finely diced and fried in a pan without fat. Add the diced paprika and the finely chopped chilli. Next, empty the egg into the pan and let it cook while stirring constantly. Sprinkle the cilantro over the scrambled eggs before serving. The protein bread can also be toasted briefly in the same pan.

Delicious ricotta and spinach frittata

332 kcal | 22.2 grams of protein | 24.4 grams of fat | 6 grams of carbohydrates **Ingredients:** 2 eggs, 30 grams of ricotta, 50 grams of tomatoes, 1 shallot, 1/4 bunch of basil, 30 grams of spinach, Himalayan salt, pepper, oil for coating the baking pan **Preparation:** Dice the shallot and tomatoes. Now roughly chop the spinach leaves and pluck the basil. Season everything with salt and pepper and mix in the ricotta. Now fill the whole thing into a lightly oiled baking dish. Then whisk the eggs and pour over this mixture. Let this bake at 180 ° Celsius for about 20 minutes.

Fresh crayfish salad with ham

369 kcal | 42.7 grams of protein | 14.4 grams of fat | 15.9 grams of carbohydrates **Ingredients:** 2 hard-boiled eggs, 20 grams of pineapple, 1/2 apple, 20 grams of crayfish, 2 slices of turkey ham, 1 tomato, 1/4 yellow pepper, 1/4 stick of celery, 2 radishes, 4 tablespoons of yogurt , Juice of an organic lemon, splash of sweetener, Himalayan salt, pepper, 1 tablespoon of chives finely

chopped **Preparation:** Mix yogurt, lemon juice, sweetener, salt, pepper and chives into a light marinade. Cut the eggs into slices and the pineapple and apple into cubes. Mix this with the diced tomato, the peppers cut into strips, and the celery and radishes cut into pieces. Now cut the ham into strips and mix together with the crayfish and the lettuce. Pour the marinade generously over the whole thing and mix it together.

Cake made from onion and egg

2,675.4 kcal | 140.8 grams of protein | 198.9 grams of fat | 61.8 grams of carbohydrates This recipe is calculated for 4

servings: **Ingredients:** 240 grams of almond flour, 120 grams of butter, 2 tablespoons of yogurt, 1 pinch of salt, 4 red onions, Himalayan salt, pepper, 6 eggs, thyme, rosemary, 200 grams of sour Cream, 3 cloves of garlic, **preparation:** Knead a shortcrust pastry from the almond flour, the butter, the yoghurt and the pinch of salt. Roll it out and put it in a round springform pan. Now pull up the edges well and prick the bottom several times with a fork. Now prebake the whole thing at 170 ° Celsius for about 10 minutes. Cut the onion and garlic into small pieces and toast them in a very little oil until golden brown. First add the herbs. Mix the eggs with the sour cream and season with salt and pepper. Finally mix with the onions. Pour the mixture into the pre-baked shortcrust pastry and bake for another 25 minutes at 160 ° Celsius.

VEGETARIAN OR DO YOU PREFER FISH?

Delicious broccoli pan served with nuts

154 kcal | 3.7 grams of protein | 9.6 grams of fat | 9 grams of carbohydrates **Ingredients:** 80 grams of broccoli, 1/4 red pepper, lemongrass, 1 chilli pepper, 5 grams of grated ginger, 1 red onion, 40 grams of green beans, 1 clove of garlic, 1 teaspoon of green curry paste, Himalayan salt, pepper, 15 grams of cashew Nuts, 3 tbsp coconut milk, 50 ml stock, 1 tbsp peanut oil **Preparation:** Finely chop the onion and garlic and sweat everything together with the ginger in a pan with a little oil. Dissolve the curry paste in it and mix this with the coconut milk. Now add the lemongrass. Chop the pepper and add it to the pan. Remove the ends and fibers from the beans, then cut them in half and add them to the pan, as well as the broccoli roses. Chop the chilli pepper and add it as well. Now season the whole thing with salt and pepper and add the broth. Let this simmer for a few minutes with the lid closed and on medium heat. Before serving, sprinkle the roasted peanuts over the dish.

Aromatic pumpkin and coconut pan

305.6 kcal | 3.5 grams of protein | 23.7 grams of fat | 22 grams of carbohydrates **Ingredients:** 150 grams of pumpkin, 30 grams of desiccated coconut, 1/2 teaspoon masala spice, 1 shallot, 1 red chilli, 1 green chilli, juice of an organic lime, 1/2 bunch of coriander, 2 lime leaves, 100 ml coconut water, 1 Teaspoon fish sauce, 1/2 teaspoon soy sauce 1 tbsp sesame oil **Preparation:** Chop the shallot and coarsely grate the pumpkin. Sweat both in oil and add the desiccated coconut. Now add the chopped chillies to the pan. Delete the whole thing with the coconut water and flavor this with the lime leaves and the masala spice. Braise this over medium heat until the liquid has evaporated. First season with the lemon juice, the fish sauce and the soy sauce. Garnish with the chopped coriander leaves.

Delicious vegetable casserole

Ingredients: 2 eggs, 1/2 carrot, 1 parsnip, 1 sweet potato, 1/2 fennel bulb, Himalayan salt, 20 ml stock, juice of an organic lime, pepper, 1 pinch of cinnamon, 1 pinch of clove powder, 1 tablespoon of sesame oil, 1 tablespoon of parsley **Preparation:** Cut the vegetables into small pieces and fry them in sesame oil in a pan. The whole thing is now deglazed with the broth and lemon juice and placed in a lightly buttered, fire-proof casserole dish. Whisk the eggs with the parsley and pour this over the vegetables. Let the vegetables and whisked eggs bake in the oven for 25 minutes at 170 ° Celsius. A small leaf salad can be served with the vegetable casserole.

Fried chicory served with cheese sauce

240.8 kcal | 16.7 grams of protein | 17.3 grams of fat | 4.5 grams of carbohydrates **Ingredients:** 2 chicory, 1 teaspoon paprika powder sweet, Himalayan salt, 1 teaspoon butter, pepper, 50 ml stock, 1 shallot, juice of an organic lime, 50 ml vegetable stock, 30 ml cream, 30 grams grated Emmentaler, 2 Spring onion, 1 tbsp olive oil **Preparation:** Cut the chicory in half and fry it on the cut surface with butter. Turn the chicory over and season it with paprika powder, salt and pepper. Now pour in the broth and leave to stand for about 3 minutes with the lid closed. First sweat the shallot in a little oil and rub it off with the lime juice. Now pour the vegetable stock on top and mix the whole thing with the cream. Fold in the grated cheese. Then it can be salted and peppered. Let the cheese melt over low heat. Now serve the chicory and cover with the cheese sauce. Finally, sprinkle the whole with the chopped spring onion.

Tofu with eggplant and zucchini

257 kcal | 26 grams of protein | 12.1 grams of fat | 7.6 grams of carbohydrates **Ingredients:** 1/2 eggplant, 1 small zucchini, olive oil for frying, Himalayan salt, pepper, 50 grams of tofu, 3 tablespoons of cream cheese, 1/2 bunch of chives, oregano, some cherry tomatoes to decorate **Preparation:** Cut the zucchini and aubergine into slices about 5 mm thick. Fry the whole thing in olive oil and season with salt and pepper. First, the vegetables are removed from the pan and dabbed off with paper towels. Now puree the tofu with cream cheese, salt, pepper, oregano and chives. Then everything can be arranged in layers. It starts with a layer of eggplant, which is coated with tofu cream. This is followed by a layer of zucchini, which is also coated with the cream again. This is repeated until everything is used up. Finally, garnish the edge of the plate with halved cherry tomatoes.

Sea bream wrapped in a banana leaf

198.4 kcal | 35 grams of protein | 5.5 grams of fat | 3 grams of carbohydrates **Ingredients:** 160 grams of sea bream fillet, juice of an organic lime, Himalayan salt, pepper, 1/2 teaspoon of yellow curry powder, 1 chopped chilli pepper, 1 egg yolk, 5 grams of ginger, 1 clove of garlic, 30 grams of yogurt, 1 banana leaf the Asia

Shop. Alternatively, just use aluminum foil. **Preparation:** Salt and pepper the fish. Mix the lime juice with the egg yolks, chopped chilli and spices. First put the garlic through the press and add it to the egg yolk. Mix the whole thing with the yoghurt and coat the whole fish fillet with this mixture on both sides. Then the coated fish fillet is wrapped in the banana leaf, placed on a baking rack and cooked at 170 ° Celsius for 25 minutes.

Perch fillet with sorrel cap

210.1 kcal | 39.1 grams of protein | 2.5 grams of fat | 8.9 grams of carbohydrates **Ingredients:** 180 grams of perch fillet, Himalayan salt, pepper, 1/2 bunch of coriander, 2 spring onions, 30 grams of sorrel (best to pick in summer and freeze in portions), 50 grams of sour cream **Preparation:** First, the fish is salted and peppered and placed in an ovenproof baking dish. Chop the spring onion and chop the coriander and sorrel. Mix the whole thing with the sour cream. Season with salt and pepper if necessary. Now the fish must be generously coated with it and cooked in the oven at 160 ° Celsius for about 15 minutes.

Exotic yellow curry with fresh pangasius and pineapple

390.2 kcal | 28.3 grams of protein | 20.5 grams of fat | 8.3 grams of carbohydrates **Ingredients:** 160 grams of pangasius, 30 grams of pineapple, 1 teaspoon of yellow curry paste, fish sauce, soy sauce, 100 ml of coconut milk, 1 chilli pepper, 1 tablespoon of chopped coriander, juice of a lime, 1 potato **Preparation:** Fry the curry paste in a Pan without oil and pour the coconut milk on it. Stir continuously to prevent lumps from forming. First peel the potato, dice it and let it cook in the coconut milk. Cut the fish into cubes and let it simmer in the coconut milk. Now dice the pineapple and add it to the pan as well. Season with fish sauce, soy sauce, chilli and lime juice. Sprinkle the dish with coriander before serving and garnish with the finely chopped chilli pepper if necessary.

Fresh king prawns with garlic oil and konjac noodles

226.2 kcal | 14.8 grams of protein | 15.9 grams of fat | 4.3 grams of carbohydrates **Ingredients:** 130 grams of konjac noodles, 3 cloves of garlic, 4 tablespoons of olive oil, 1 chilli pepper, 130 grams of king prawns, Himalayan salt, pepper, parsley for sprinkling **Preparation:** Finely chop the garlic cloves and then roast them in olive oil at. The chilli pepper is also cut into small pieces and added to the garlic. First fry the king prawns in garlic oil and season them with salt and pepper. Take the king prawns out of the pan. Briefly wash the konjac noodles with hot water and then toss them in the pan with the garlic oil. Arrange the pasta on a plate, place the king prawns on top and sprinkle everything with parsley.

Grilled bell peppers with monkfish wrapped in bacon

479.1 kcal | 47.1 grams of protein | 28.6 grams of fat | 6.6 grams of carbohydrates **Ingredients:** 180 grams of monkfish, 4 thin slices of bacon, Himalayan salt, pepper, juice of an organic lemon, 1/2 red pepper, 1/2 yellow pepper, 1/2 green pepper, 2 tbsp olive oil **Preparation:** Salt, pepper and sour the fish and wrap the bacon around it. First fry the whole thing in a pan with olive oil. Then finish cooking in the oven at 120 ° Celsius for 15 minutes. Cut the peppers into wide strips and fry them in olive oil. Finally, the whole thing is salted and peppered and served on the plate. Now put the fish on top and enjoy.

SNACKS & SIDE DISHES

Are you looking for low carb recipes for a snack in between meals? We have something for you. It is important that you pay attention to how you combine the snacks and side dishes with the total daily turnover of carbohydrates. Calories and fat are not in the foreground in a low carb diet - this means that you don't have to go hungry and still lose pounds in no time.

Humus in combination with celery

131.2 kcal | Protein: 9.2 grams | Fat: 2.8 grams | Carbohydrates: 17.3

grams **Preparation time:** 6 minutes **Ingredients:** 80 grams of canned chickpeas | 2 cloves of garlic | 2 tbsp cottage cheese | 1 chilli pepper | 2 tbsp orange juice with no added sugar | Salt and pepper | 2 stalks of celery **Preparation:** Strain the chickpeas and put them in the blender along with the garlic, cottage cheese, chilli and orange juice. Then season the paste with salt and pepper. Now the celery can be cut into pieces and dipped into the humus. You can also eat this humus as a spread on a slice of protein bread.

Small low carb pizza made from eggplant

97.8 kcal | Protein: 8.3 grams | Fat: 5.8 grams | Carbohydrates: 3.1 grams **Preparation time:** 12 minutes **Ingredients:** 4 slices of eggplant approx. 1 cm thick 3 tbsp pizza tomatoes with no added sugar | 20 grams of Gouda | Oregano | Salt and pepper | 2 tablespoons of canned tuna - in its own juice **Preparation:** To start, fry the aubergines in a grill pan without oil on both sides. Take this out of the pan and place the aubergines on a baking sheet lined with baking paper. The whole thing can now be salted, peppered and coated with the pizza tomatoes. Sprinkle everything with Gouda cheese and season with oregano, salt and pepper. First cover the slices with tuna and bake at 200 ° Celsius for 6 minutes with top and bottom heat. There are no limits to your imagination when it comes to topping the pizzas.

Delicious zucchini sticks

185.8 kcal | Protein: 11.6 grams | Fat: 14.6 grams | Carbohydrates: 2 grams **Preparation time:** 7 minutes **Ingredients:** 1/2 zucchini | 1 egg | 2 tbsp almond flour | 2 tbsp yogurt | Salt and pepper | Oil for deep-frying **Preparation:** To start, cut the zucchini into sticks and season with salt and pepper. Whisk the egg with the almond flour and yogurt. Now pull the sticks through and bake in hot oil. Alternatively, they can also be fried in the deep fryer or in the oven.

Fresh carrot cakes

141.8 kcal | Protein: 12.6 grams | Fat: 7.4 grams | Carbohydrates: 6.2 grams **Preparation time:** 8 minutes **Ingredients:** 1/2 carrot | 1 egg | 2 tbsp almond flour | Salt and pepper | grated some nutmeg **Preparation:**

First, beat the egg until frothy and finely grate the carrot. Now you can mix the almond flour with the egg and stir in the grated carrot. Season the whole thing with salt, pepper and nutmeg and bake small pancakes in a non-stick pan.

Omelette with honey ham

225.2 kcal | Protein: 17.9 grams | Fat: 16.4 grams | Carbohydrates: 1.5 grams **Preparation time:** 6 minutes **Ingredients:** 60 grams of honey ham (1 slice) | 1 egg | some thyme | 2 tbsp milk | 1 tbsp chives in rolls | Salt and pepper **Preparation:** Whisk the egg with the thyme, milk and chives and then season with salt and pepper. Pull the ham through the egg and fry it in a coated pan. Now pour the rest of the egg over it. Let the egg set and turn everything carefully. If you like, mix grated cheese into the egg.

Low carb fries made from carrots and cheese

115 kcal | Protein: 6.4 grams | Fat: 7.8 grams | Carbohydrates: 4.8 grams **Preparation time:** 15 minutes **Ingredients:** 1 carrot | 1 tbsp olive oil | Salt and pepper | 20 grams of grated cheese **Preparation:** Cut the carrot into sticks about 0.5 cm thick and then place them on a baking sheet lined with baking paper. Now drizzle the sticks with the olive oil and add a little salt and pepper. Preheat the oven to 170 ° Celsius and bake the fries on top and bottom heat for 8 minutes. Finally, sprinkle the sticks with the cheese and let them bake for another 5 minutes.

Bell peppers baked with melted camembert

132.5 kcal | Protein: 12.7 grams | Fat: 6.5 grams | Carbohydrates: 5.8 grams **Preparation time:** 7 minutes **Ingredients:** 1/2 yellow pepper | 1/2 red pepper | 30 grams of blackberries | 50 grams of camembert | Freshly ground pepper **Preparation:** Cut the peppers into 2 cm thick strips. Next, line a baking sheet with parchment paper and spread the peppers on top. Now top with the blackberries and cover with the sliced camembert. Preheat the oven to 200 ° Celsius and bake the peppers on top and bottom heat for about 4 to 5 minutes.

Green asparagus with a fruity strawberry dip

196.8 kcal | Protein: 13.5 grams | Fat: 14 grams | Carbohydrates: 4.2 grams

Preparation time: 10 minutes **Ingredients:** 4 stalks of green asparagus | 1 tbsp almond flour | 1 egg | 2 tbsp almonds grated | Salt and pepper | 3 strawberries | 1 tbsp quark **Preparation:** At the beginning, cut off the lower ends of the asparagus and halve the asparagus lengthways. Then roll this in almond flour. Whisk the egg with salt and pepper and pull the asparagus through. Next, bread this in the almonds and place on a baking sheet lined with baking paper. Now bake the whole thing at 160 ° Celsius and top and bottom heat for 6 minutes. Mash the strawberries with a fork or magic wand, mix them with the quark and sprinkle the dip with a little pepper.

Cream cheese bacon pancakes

274.1 kcal | Protein: 24.5 grams | Fat: 17.7 grams | Carbohydrates: 4.2 grams

Preparation time: 10 minutes **Ingredients:** 2 eggs | 50 ml low-fat milk | 2 tbsp almond flour | Salt and pepper | 1 tbsp parsley chopped | 2 tbsp cream cheese | 2 tbsp bacon diced. **Preparation:** Whisk eggs with milk and then stir in almond flour. Season the whole thing with salt and pepper and add the parsley. Now the dough can be processed into thin pancakes, so-called pancakes, in a coated pan without oil. Take the pancakes out of the pan and coat them with cream cheese. Now spread the bacon on top. Beat in the pancakes and place them on a baking sheet. Let the whole thing bake at 180 ° Celsius for 3 minutes with top and bottom heat.

BEEF, POULTRY, PIG OR BUT LAMB?

Kohlrabi vegetables with a juicy saddle of veal

324.8 kcal | 33 grams of protein | 17.5 grams of fat | 6.3 grams of carbohydrates **Ingredients:** 180 grams of veal saddle, 100 ml of veal stock, 150 grams of kohlrabi, 1 teaspoon wasabi paste, 50 grams of sour cream, 1 tablespoon of coriander, 1 tablespoon of watercress, Himalayan salt, pepper, 1 pinch of ground cumin, oil for Searing **Preparation:** Cut the veal into 1 cm thick slices, fry it in a little oil and season with salt and pepper. Now the calf has to be kept warm in the oven at 60 ° Celsius. Cut the kohlrabi into small cubes and sweat it in a pan. Then add the stock and cook until al dente. First stir in the wasabi paste and bind the whole thing with the sour cream. Now flavor the dish with the coriander, caraway seeds and watercress. Put the vegetables in a soup plate and serve the veal on top.

Beef roulade (baked)

284.2 kcal | 41.4 grams of protein | 13.4 grams of fat | 2.1 grams of carbohydrates **Ingredients:** 200 grams of beef from the topside, 1 teaspoon of mustard, 1/4 carrot, 1 pickle, 1 slice of bacon, 1/4 stick of celery, Himalayan salt, pepper, 1 teaspoon of tomato paste, 200 ml of broth, 2 Juniper berries, 1 bay leaf, 1 sprig of thyme, 1 sprig of rosemary, oil for frying **Preparation:** Knock the beef schnitzel very thinly and coat it with a thin layer of mustard. First, salt and pepper. Now the vegetables must be cut into sticks and placed on the end of the schnitzel. Then put the bacon on top and roll up the meat. Fix the whole thing with a toothpick. The meat can now be fried all around in oil and the tomato paste added. Roast this briefly and pour the broth on everything. Finally, add the herbs and spices. Finally, the dish is baked in the oven for 1 hour at 150 ° Celsius.

Beef fillet pan served with sugar snap peas

289.7 kcal | 42.1 grams of protein | 7.9 grams of fat | 14.6 grams of carbohydrates **Ingredients:** 150 grams of beef fillet, 1/2 red onion, 2 cloves of garlic, 100 grams of snow peas, 100 grams of Swiss chard, juice of an organic lime, 1 tbsp soy sauce, 1/2 bunch of mint, Himalayan salt, pepper, oil for Searing **Preparation:** Cut the fillet into strips and fry it in a little oil. Then the fillet can be removed from the pan and dabbed with kitchen paper. Finely dice the onion and garlic, sauté them and add the sugar snap peas. Roughly cut the Swiss chard and add this to the pan as well. First season with salt and pepper and add the soy sauce to taste. Add the lime juice and then place the beef back in the pan. Finally mix everything together and serve. Garnish with the chopped mint before serving.

Delicious beef meatballs in an aromatic curry sauce

295 kcal | 29.9 grams of protein | 16.5 grams of fat | 7.4 grams of carbohydrates **Ingredients:** 100 grams of ground beef, 1/2 teaspoon mustard, 1 tablespoon of almond flour, Himalayan salt, pepper, 1

teaspoon of chopped parsley, 15 grams of chopped hazelnuts, oil for frying, 1 shallot, 1 clove of garlic, 1 teaspoon of yellow curry powder , 30 ml broth, 30 ml cream, 50 grams leek **Preparation:** Mix ground beef with mustard, almond flour, parsley and nuts and season everything with salt and pepper. First form small balls with wet hands. Fry the balls in hot oil on all sides and then remove them from the fat. First let the whole thing drain well and dab with kitchen paper. Now finish cooking in the oven at 150 ° Celsius for 10 minutes. Sweat the chopped onions and chopped garlic in the pan. Next, cut the leek into thin rings and add to it. Sprinkle the whole thing with curry powder and then pour the broth over it. Now season with salt and pepper and refine with the cream. Finally, put the balls in the pan, toss them briefly and serve.

Delicious carpaccio served with parmesan, tomatoes and dried apricots

388.6 kcal | 31.8 grams of protein | 26.4 grams of fat | 3.4 grams of carbohydrates **Ingredients:** 120 grams of beef fillet, 30 grams of parmesan, 1 tomato, 2 dried apricots without added sugar, 1 tablespoon of pine nuts, 20 grams of rocket, 3 tablespoons of olive oil,

2 tablespoons of balsamic vinegar dark, Himalayan salt, milled pepper , Juice of an organic lemon **Preparation:** Cut the beef fillet into very thin slices and carefully pound this under a cling film until it is very thin. Now the slices are arranged on a plate and drizzled with olive oil and balsamic vinegar. Grate the parmesan cheese on top and season with salt and pepper. Put the rocket on top and marinate everything with a few squirts of lemon juice. Finally, finely dice the apricots and spread them over the dish together with the pine nuts.

Lemon-ginger-flavored chicken

444.7 kcal | 55.9 grams of protein | 21.5 grams of fat | 0.5 grams of carbohydrates **Ingredients:** 180 grams of chicken fillet, 5 grams of freshly grated ginger, juice and zest of two organic lemons, 1 pinch of aniseed seeds, 1 pinch of coriander seeds, thyme, Himalayan salt, pepper, 2 tablespoons of olive oil **Preparation:** Rub that Put the chicken fillet with the spices, ginger and zest from the lemons. Then place on a baking sheet and drizzle with lemon juice and olive oil. First, put the sprig of thyme on the meat. Then let the whole thing cook in the oven at 160 ° Celsius for 20 minutes.

Turkey roll roast on fresh spinach leaves

993.6 kcal | 126.9 grams of protein | 49.3 grams of fat | 9.3 grams of

carbohydrates The recipe is calculated for 2 servings: **Ingredients:** 500 grams of turkey breast, 80 grams of spinach leaves, 30 grams of walnuts, 30 grams of blue cheese, oil for frying, Himalayan salt, pepper, 80 ml of cream, 200 ml of broth, thyme **Preparation:** Beat the turkey breast. Salt and pepper this and brush the blue cheese on one side. Now sprinkle the turkey breast with the roughly chopped nuts. First, briefly blanch the spinach leaves and place on the turkey. Next, the whole thing is rolled up and fixed with a kitchen thread. Fry the turkey roll on all sides and pour the stock into the pan. Now add the thyme and cook in the oven for 40 minutes at 150 ° Celsius. Then take the roast out of the pan and keep it warm in the oven. Let the stock reduce in the pan over medium heat and refine it with the cream. Season to taste and serve with the slices of roast.

Delicious Chicken Salad Hula Hula (Hawaiian Style)

425.7 kcal | 44.9 grams of protein | 17.4 grams of fat | 16.6 grams of

carbohydrates **Ingredients:** 100 grams of chicken, 100 grams of turkey, 50 grams of pineapple, 50 grams of peach (fresh or canned with no added sugar), 1/2 stick of celery, 1 tomato, 1/2 yellow pepper, juice of an organic Lemon, 3 tablespoons of yogurt, 1 tablespoon of sour cream, 2 tablespoons of olive oil, Himalayan salt, pepper, 1 slice of protein bread, 100 grams of rocket **Preparation:** Cut the poultry into strips and fry them in a pan without fat. Now the fruits and vegetables have to be cut into bite-sized pieces. Yoghurt, sour cream, olive oil, salt and pepper make the marinade. Mix the meat with the cut fruits and vegetables and then mix this with the dressing. The whole thing is now served on the rocket salad and flavored with a few squirts of lemon juice. A slice of protein bread goes wonderfully with it. If necessary, this can be processed into croutons in a coated pan. Then simply sprinkle over the salad.

Delicious meatballs made from chicken and mozzarella

341 kcal | 46.8 grams of protein | 12.6 grams of fat | 5.9 grams of carbohydrates **Ingredients:** 100 grams of minced chicken, 1 egg, thyme, Himalayan salt, pepper, 1/2 teaspoon mustard, 30 grams of mozzarella, oil for frying, 1 shallot, 1 clove of garlic, 2 tomatoes, 1/2 zucchini, Rosemary, basil **Preparation:** Process the minced chicken with salt, pepper, thyme, mustard and the egg into a smooth mass. Shape these into two balls and place half of the mozzarella in the middle. Cover with the meat and form a loaf. Now fry them well in

oil on both sides. First, sauté the chopped shallots and garlic in a second pan. Then add the chopped zucchini and tomatoes. Season the whole thing with rosemary, basil, salt and pepper and let everything cook. Now everything can be served together with the meatballs.

Juicy turkey medallions on braised radishes

284.7 kcal | 37.8 grams of protein | 12 grams of fat | 5.6 grams of carbohydrates **Ingredients:** 150 grams turkey breast thereof cut 3 medallions, 1/2 bunch radishes, 1/2 vanilla bean, thyme, sage, 50 ml broth, 50 ml sour cream, Himalaya salt, pepper, 2 tablespoons butter **Preparation:** salts and pepper the medallions and fry them in butter. Then remove from the pan and set aside. Now the radishes have to be quartered and tossed in the frying pan. First, salt and pepper the whole thing. With thyme, sage and the pulp of the vanilla pod you give the dish a great aroma. Now pour in the broth, sauté briefly and refine with the sour cream. Finally, the medallions can be returned to the pan, swirled briefly and served.

October Schnitzel (Munich style)

742.5 kcal | 57.1 grams of protein | 50 grams of fat | 12.2 grams of carbohydrates **Ingredients:** 150 grams of pork tenderloin, 1 tablespoon of sweet mustard, 10 grams of freshly grated horseradish, 20 grams of almond flour, 1 egg, 60 grams of roughly chopped nuts, Himalayan salt, pepper, oil for deep-frying **Preparation:** Cut the pork tenderloin into Medallions and then pat it thin. Now salt and pepper and coat one side with the sweet mustard. Spread the horseradish on top. Roll the whole thing in almond flour, pull it through the beaten egg and bread it in the nuts. Finally, bake in the oil and then drain well on a paper towel.

Cheese skewers in different colors

388.9 kcal | 44.3 grams of protein | 20.2 grams of fat | 6.6 grams of carbohydrates

Ingredients: 130 grams of pork tenderloin, 2 cubes of goat cheese each 10 grams, 4 cocktail tomatoes, 1/4 yellow pepper, 1/4 green pepper, 1/2 onion, 2 cloves of garlic, 4 slices of zucchini, 2 slices of eggplant, Himalayan salt , Pepper **Preparation:** Cut the meat into pieces of the same size and alternately fill two skewers with meat and vegetables. Then the skewers must be salted, peppered and fried in a grill pan without fat. Alternatively, you can grill them on the grill. The skewers can be conjured up at will. You can use all kinds of meat and vegetables. Let your creativity take over your mind and body.

Grilled pork chops with low carb salsa

466.2 kcal | 44.3 grams of protein | 28.6 grams of fat | 8.5 grams of carbohydrates **Ingredients:** pork chops with bone approx. 230 grams, 1 clove of garlic, Himalayan salt, pepper, rosemary, 2 tablespoons of oil, 2 tablespoons of butter **Preparation:** Season the meat with salt and pepper and fry it in hot oil at. First remove the fat from the pan and add the butter to the pan. Let the meat cook with the garlic and rosemary in the pan over medium heat. Pour the butter over the meat several times with a spoon. Serve the pork chops with some salsa.

Hearty pork goulash

306.6 kcal | 33.6 grams of protein | 8.1 grams of fat | 22.9 grams of carbohydrates **Ingredients:** 150 grams of the pork shell, 60 grams of peeled chestnuts, 1/2 onion, 20 grams of bacon, oil for frying, Himalayan salt, pepper 1 bay leaf, 150 ml stock, thyme, marjoram, 1/2 tsp Sweet paprika powder, 1 pinch of hot paprika powder, 1 dash of red wine vinegar **Preparation:** Cut the meat into cubes and fry it in hot fat along with the chopped onion and bacon. Add chestnuts and season with salt and pepper. First sprinkle paprika powder over it. Deglaze everything with vinegar and pour the broth over the dish. Then add the thyme, rosemary and bay leaf to the broth and simmer for an hour with the lid closed over medium heat.

Delicious pork medallions served with fresh mushrooms and peppers

374.8 kcal | 35.1 grams of protein | 22 grams of fat | 6.5 grams of carbohydrates **Ingredients:** 150 grams of pork tenderloin, 1 shallot, 1/2 red pepper, 60 grams of mushrooms, 1 clove of garlic, 1/2 teaspoon of tomato paste, Himalayan salt, pepper, 50 ml stock, 30 ml cream, marjoram, 1 pinch Ground caraway seeds, 2 tbsp butter **Preparation:** Cut the fillet into medallions and flatten them lightly. Then the medallions are salted and peppered. Chop the shallots and garlic and cut the mushrooms and peppers into strips. First fry the meat on both sides in the butter and then remove it from the pan. Garlic, schallots, peppers and mushrooms are then fried in the same pan. Toast the tomato paste lightly. First add marjoram and caraway seeds and pour the stock on top. Let this simmer for 5 minutes and then refine it with the cream. Finally, season with salt and pepper and let the meat soak in the sauce for 3 minutes.

Delicious truffled celery vegetables with lamb fillet

370.3 kcal | 19 grams of protein | 30.2 grams of fat | 2.9 grams of carbohydrates

Ingredients: 130 grams of lamb fillet, 100 grams of celery, 1 shallot, 1 clove of garlic, Himalayan salt, pepper, grated nutmeg. Thyme, rosemary, 1 tbsp parsley finely chopped, 1 tbsp butter, 1 tbsp truffle oil, oil for frying **Preparation:** Salt and pepper the lamb fillet and stick a sprig of rosemary in the middle of the meat. A tiny cut can be made in the meat for this. Fry the meat in hot oil on all sides and let it finish cooking in the oven at 100 ° Celsius for 20 minutes. Dice the celery and let it boil briefly in salted water. First chop the shallot and garlic and sauté in butter. Add the cooked celery. Now season the dish with salt, pepper, nutmeg, thyme and parsley. Finally refine with truffle oil and serve with the meat.

Delicious chestnut puree on lamb chops

789.4 kcal | 33.3 grams of protein | 50.8 grams of fat | 47.3 grams of carbohydrates **Ingredients:** 130 grams of minced lamb, 1/2 onion, 1 clove of garlic, 1/2 teaspoon of chopped parsley, mugwort, 1/2 teaspoon of mustard, 1 egg, Himalayan salt, cayenne pepper, 1 tablespoon of almond flour, 100 grams Chestnuts, 1 tbsp butter, 50 ml cream, pulp of half a vanilla pod **Preparation:** Finely chop the onion and garlic and sweat everything in butter. Then mix this with the minced lamb and parsley. First whisk an egg with almond flour and knead with the meat. Now season this with mustard, salt and cayenne pepper and shape it into patties. Fry them in a pan with a little oil, turning several times. Now boil the chestnuts in salted water with the pulp of the vanilla pod until soft, strain and puree with the butter and cream. Finally, season the chestnut puree with salt and pepper and serve.

Juicy lamb chop with fried apple

550.9 kcal | 27.5 grams of protein | 40.3 grams of fat | 16.2 grams of carbohydrates **Ingredients:** 200 grams of bone chops, 1 apple, 2 cloves of garlic, Himalayan salt, pepper, thyme, 2 tablespoons of olive oil, oil for frying, 2 tablespoons of red balsamic vinegar, 30 grams of bacon, 2 cloves **Preparation:** Fry Sear the chops in oil on both sides. While the chops are frying in the pan, a marinade can now be prepared from garlic, salt, pepper, olive oil and thyme. First, core the apple and sprinkle with the cloves. Take the pork chops out of the pan and place them in an ovenproof casserole dish. Cover this with the bacon. Put the apple next to it and fill it with 2/3 of the marinade. Then drizzle the remaining marinade over the meat. Let the dish simmer in the oven for 30 minutes at 120 ° Celsius. After 15 minutes, add the balsamic vinegar to everything.

Delicious Mediterranean lamb fillet

433.2 kcal | 22.8 grams of protein | 33 grams of fat | 7.3 grams of carbohydrates **Ingredients:** 130 lamb salmon or loin, 1 shallot, 1/4 zucchini, 1/4 yellow pepper, 1/4 aubergine, 2 cloves of garlic, oregano, thyme, rosemary, 4 cherry tomatoes, 2 tbsp balsamic vinegar, 2 Tablespoons olive oil, Himalayan salt, pepper, zest of an organic orange **Preparation:** Cut the meat into 1 cm thick strips and the vegetables into pieces of the same size. First, roughly chop the garlic and shallot. Sear the meat in the olive oil and remove it from the pan. Now add onion, garlic and paprika and roast it together. Then zucchini and eggplant can be added. Then season the whole thing with the herbs and then rub it off with the balsamic vinegar. Now add the meat again. Pierce the tomatoes with a fork and then add them to the pan as well. Then everything can be flavored with the zest of the organic orange. Finally let the dish stew in the oven for 20 minutes at 170 ° Celsius

DESSERTS

Baked vanilla ice cream in a meringue coating

178.4 kcal | Protein: 5.5 grams | Fat: 4.8 grams | Carbohydrates: 28.3 grams **Preparation time:** 8 minutes **Ingredients:** 1 nectarine | 2 small scoops of low carb vanilla ice cream | 1 egg white | 1 tbsp xylitol or sweetener **Preparation:** Halve and core the nectarine at the beginning. Put a scoop of ice cream in each well. Now the egg white with the sweetener can be beaten to a stiff snow and the nectarine and the ice can be coated with it. Now place this on a baking sheet lined with baking paper and preheat the oven to 220 ° Celsius. Bake the dessert on top and bottom heat for 3 minutes. Finally, take it out of the oven and enjoy immediately.

Delicious low carb frozen yogurt

236.2 kcal | Protein: 11.2 grams | Fat: 14.2 grams | Carbohydrates: 15.9 grams **Preparation time:** 8 minutes Freezing time: 6 hours **Ingredients:** 120 grams of yoghurt | 1 egg white | 1 tbsp xylitol or sweetener | Pulp of half a vanilla pod | some abrasion of an untreated organic lime | 50 ml cream **Preparation:** Mix the yoghurt with the egg white, sweetener, vanilla and zest. Then whip the cream until stiff and fold it under. Now pour the mixture into a bowl and freeze for at least 6 hours. Take this out of the freezer and use the mixer to make a frozen yoghurt. Garnish with fresh berries if you like.

Delicious gratinated berries

117.5 kcal | Protein: 5.9 grams | Fat: 4.7 grams | Carbohydrates: 12.9 grams **Preparation time:** 10 minutes **Ingredients:** 80 grams of fresh or frozen berry mix | 1 egg | Juice and zest of half an untreated organic orange | 1 teaspoon xylitol, stevia or sweetener as required **Preparation:** Beat the egg with the orange juice and the sweetener over a hot water bath until frothy. Put the berries in a small baking dish and marinate them with the zest. Now pour the egg mixture over the whole thing. Preheat the oven to 220 ° Celsius and grill the berries on top and bottom heat for 4 minutes.

Apple crumble with delicious low carb sprinkles

273.4 kcal | Protein: 11.2 grams | Fat: 20.2 grams | Carbohydrates: 11.7 grams **Preparation time:** 12 minutes **Ingredients:** 1/2 apple | 1 squirt of lemon juice | 20 grams of butter | 30 grams of almond flour

| 1 pinch of cinnamon | some abrasion of an untreated organic orange | Sweetener as required **Preparation:** Cut the apple into thin wedges and layer them in a small tart form. Now drizzle the whole thing with the lemon juice. Melt the butter in a pan and stir in the almond flour along with the cinnamon and sweetener. Stir until the mixture loosens crumbly from the bottom of the pan. Spread the crumbs over the apples, flavor everything with the zest and put the tart pan in the oven. Now bake at 180 ° Celsius for 10 minutes with top and bottom heat.

Exotic low carb protein shake

Calories: 154.5 kcal | Protein: 4.2 grams | Fat: 6.5 grams | Carbohydrates: 19.8 grams Preparation time: 5 minutes **Ingredients:** 1/2 mango | 30 grams of papaya | Juice and zest of half an untreated organic lime | 100 ml orange juice freshly squeezed or with no added sugar | 50 ml coconut milk | 1 teaspoon whey powder | Sweetener or stevia as required. **Preparation:** This shake can be prepared in no time at all. Put all the ingredients in a blender and mix everything well. This shake is also very suitable as a breakfast shake. You can add a spoonful of wheat bran to the shake for this. Finally, sweeten as you like ..

Heavenly low carb brownies

2972.3 kcal | Protein: 47.5 grams | Fat: 187.5 grams | Carbohydrates: 273.7 grams

Preparation time: 25 minutes **Ingredients for approx. 12 brownies:** 120 grams of butter | 3 eggs | 250 grams of dark chocolate xylitol | 80 grams of xylitol or stevia as required | 60 grams of almond flour | 2 tbsp double-defoiled cocoa | 1 pack of baking powder | 1 pinch of Himalayan rock salt **Preparation:** Beat the butter until foamy and stir one egg after the other into the butter. Melt the chocolate in a small pan, stirring constantly, and then stir it quickly into the butter mixture. First add the sweetener, almond flour, cocoa, baking powder and salt. Pour the batter into a lightly buttered baking dish. Heat the oven to 175 ° Celsius and bake the brownies on top and bottom heat for 20 minutes. Now take it out of the oven and cut into 12 pieces.

Dream muffins with vanilla and ginger

943.1 kcal | Protein: 43.3 grams | Fat: 81.1 grams | Carbohydrates: 10 grams

Preparation time: 20 minutes **Ingredients for 4 muffins:** 2 eggs | 90 grams of almond flour | 1 pack of baking powder | 3 tbsp Greek yogurt | Pulp of a vanilla pod or vanilla flavor | 1 pinch of freshly grated ginger or powder | 2 tbsp chopped walnuts | 4 walnut halves **Preparation:** Separate the eggs and use the whisk or hand mixer to work the egg white into a stiff snow. Mix the egg yolks with the Greek yogurt and work in the almond flour and baking powder. First stir in the vanilla, ginger and chopped walnuts and then carefully fold in the egg whites. Fill the batter into four muffin tins. Put one walnut half on each muffin. Heat the oven to 170 ° Celsius and bake the muffins on top and bottom heat for about 15 minutes.

Low carb chocolate ice cream

Calories: 1130.2 kcal | Protein: 26.3 grams | Fat: 66.6 grams | Carbohydrates: 106.4 grams **Preparation time:** 10 minutes Freezing time: at least 6 hours **Ingredients for four servings:** 2 eggs | 1 egg white | 100 grams of dark chocolate xylitol | 2 tbsp xylitol, stevia or sweetener | 200 ml cream **Preparation:** At the beginning, beat the eggs with the sweetener until frothy and then stir in the egg white. Let the chocolate melt under a hot water bath. Quickly stir this into the egg mixture with the whisk. Now whip the cream until stiff and fold in carefully. Pour the mass into a tub and freeze it for at least 6 hours. Take the tub out of the freezer and take a total of 4 servings of ice from the mixture.

Fresh crepes with delicious berry sauce

Calories: 418.6 kcal | Protein: 17.1 grams | Fat: 33.4 grams
| Carbohydrates: 12.4 grams **Preparation time:** 9
minutes **Ingredients for one serving:** 2 egg yolks | 60 ml cream | 2
tbsp coconut flour | 1 pinch of Himalayan salt | 50 grams of wild
berries fresh or frozen | 2 tbsp cottage cheese | 1 teaspoon xylitol or
sweetener | some abrasion of an untreated organic
orange **Preparation:** Whisk egg yolks with cream and mix everything
with coconut flour and salt. In a non-stick pan, bake the batter into
thin crepes. With the help of a magic wand, puree the berries along
with the cottage cheese, sweetener and zest. Pour the sauce over the
crepes. Sprinkle with a little powdered xylitol or garnish with a dollop
of cream.

Refreshing yogurt pudding

Calories: 163.6 kcal | Protein: 12.4 grams | Fat: 6.8 grams
| Carbohydrates: 13.2 grams **Preparation time:** 8 minutes Cooling
time: at least 4 hours **Ingredients for one serving:** 150 grams of
yoghurt | 1 tsp chia seeds | 1 tbsp xylitol or sweetener | some vanilla

flavor | some abrasion of an untreated organic lime | 50 ml freshly squeezed grapefruit juice | 1 pinch of instant gelatine **Preparation:** Mix the yoghurt with the chia seeds, the sweetener, the vanilla and the lime zest. Pour the mixture into a glass. Mix the grapefruit juice with the instant gelatin until it has completely dissolved. Now spread the whole thing over the yoghurt and let it set in the refrigerator for at least 4 hours, preferably overnight.

Carrot muffins with cinnamon and cocoa

Calories: 964.4 kcal | Protein: 49.8 grams | Fat: 77.6 grams | Carbohydrates: 16.7 grams **Preparation time:** 20 minutes **Ingredients for 4 muffins:** 60 grams of butter | 2 eggs | 2 tbsp yogurt | 90 grams of almond flour | 1/2 pack of baking powder | 100 grams of carrots finely grated | 2 tbsp finely chopped pistachios | 1 pinch of cinnamon | 1 tbsp double-defoiled cocoa | 1 pinch of Himalayan salt | 2 dashes of sweetener **Preparation:** Beat the butter until frothy and stir one egg after the other into the butter. Work in almond flour, baking powder, yogurt, carrots, pistachios, cinnamon, cocoa, salt and sweetener. Divide the mixture into four muffin tins. Now bake the muffins at 180 ° Celsius with top and bottom heat for 15 minutes.

MIXTURES AND SNACKS FOR IN-BETWEEN

Especially between meals it can happen that you get hungry and you could tolerate a snack. However, it doesn't hurt to ask yourself briefly whether you are really hungry enough for a snack. It might as well be that you are just thirsty, as thirst often shows symptoms similar to hunger. In this case, drink a glass of water with a squirt of lemon juice. This refreshes and is good for your body. If the symptoms persist, there are great, simple, and healthy snack alternatives.

Hearty egg custard

178.9 kcal | 14.6 grams of protein | 13 grams of fat | 1.2 grams of carbohydrates **Ingredients:** 2 eggs, 100 ml vegetable stock, 1/2 chilli pepper, 1 pinch of Himalayan salt, pepper, 1 dash of vinegar **Preparation:** Cut the chilli peppers into small pieces and mix with the remaining ingredients. Then put everything in an ovenproof bowl and place it in a deep pan filled with water. Then put both together in the oven at 170 ° Celsius for 30 minutes. There are no limits to creativity with this snack either. As long as the ingredients contain little or no carbohydrates, you can add anything you like.

Healthy cheese chips for in between

430 kcal | 37 grams of protein | 29 grams of fat | 2 grams of carbohydrates **Ingredients:** 100 grams of Parmesan or particularly hard grated cheese, 1 sprig of rosemary **Preparation:** Grate the cheese and mix with the finely chopped rosemary. Then shape small balls out of the cheese and place them on a baking sheet lined with baking paper. Then bake the cheese balls in the oven at 200 ° for about 10 minutes until they are crispy and golden yellow.

Cauliflower Muffins

1 macaroon has about: 24.8 kcal | 2 grams of protein | 1.7 grams of fat | 0.5 grams of carbohydrates **Ingredients:** 1/2 cauliflower, 100 grams of cheese, 30 grams of almond flour, 1 chilli pepper, 5 grams of grated ginger, 2 eggs, Himalayan salt, **Preparation:** Put half of the cauliflower together with the other ingredients in the blender and good mix. Remove the florets from the other half of the cauliflower

and add them to the mixed ingredients. Then put everything in muffin molds and bake at 200 ° for 15 minutes. Turn the macaroons occasionally so that they bake evenly. Then leave in the oven for another 15 minutes. The cauliflower muffin is also perfect for parties. The preparation is quick and the muffins are super healthy and delicious. The healthy alternative for your party!

Delicious cream cheese balls

562 kcal | 39.6 grams of protein | 32.1 grams of fat | 21.4 grams of carbohydrates **Ingredients:** 300 grams of cream cheese, finely chopped herbs, crushed peppercorns, finely chopped nuts, finely chopped yellow peppers **Preparation:** Form small balls out of the cream cheese and roll them in the various ingredients. The different variations give your snack a colorful variety and variety and are also ideal for parties.

Styrian potato cheese

243 kcal | 4.8 grams of protein | 16.4 grams of fat | 17.8 grams of carbohydrates **Ingredients:** 100 grams of potatoes, 50 grams of sour cream or sour cream, 1 shallot, Himalayan salt, pepper, 1 teaspoon of pumpkin seed oil, 1 tablespoon of chopped pumpkin seeds **Preparation:** Put the potatoes unpeeled in the saucepan and let

it boil. Then peel and press into a mash. This works best with a potato press. But it also works well with a fork. Only the mixer is not suitable for this. Then cut the shallots into small pieces and add them to the mashed potatoes. Now add the remaining ingredients and enjoy the potato cheese as a dip or as a spread!

Zucchini sticks prepared in the oven

245 kcal | 20 grams of protein | 15 grams of fat | 4.2 grams of carbohydrates **Ingredients:** 1 zucchini, 50 grams of Parmesan, oregano, thyme, Himalayan salt, pepper, 2 tablespoons of vinegar **Preparation:** Cut small strips or sticks from the zucchini and remove the seeds. Then spread the vinegar with it and season with salt and pepper. Mix the parmesan with herbs and sprinkle on the zucchini. Bake the sticks in the oven at 170 ° for 15 minutes.

BEVERAGES

Low carb protein shake

182.6 kcal | Protein: 17.3 grams | Fat: 7.8 grams | Carbohydrates: 10.8 grams **Preparation time:** 5 minutes **Ingredients for one serving:** 200 grams of kefir | 1 egg white | 1 tbsp vanilla flavored whey powder | Sweetener as required **Preparation:** Mix all ingredients in a blender to make a creamy smoothie. First beat the egg white to a stiff snow and stir it with kefir until smooth. Now work in the whey powder quickly. Which type of whey powder is up to you

Mango and ginger in a green smoothie

32.1 kcal | Protein: 0.7 grams | Fat: 0.1 grams | Carbohydrates: 7.1 grams

Preparation time: 3 minutes **Ingredients for one serving** : 150 ml cold green tea | 1 cm fresh ginger | 1 splash of lime juice | 1/2 mango | Sweetener or stevia as required. **Preparation:** Put all the ingredients in the blender and mix everything into a creamy shake. All other types of tea can also be used for this drink, such as various herbal teas. A few ice cubes can also be added to the blender on hot days. This will give you a refreshing slushy.

Water flavored with melon

53.9 kcal | Protein: 0.9 grams | Fat: 0.3 grams | Carbohydrates: 11.9 grams **Preparation time:** 2 minutes **Ingredients for one serving:** 1 liter of water, mineral water or soda water | 150 grams of watermelon seedless | 1/2 bunch of mint | Lemon juice | Sweetener as required **Preparation:** Cut the watermelon into large pieces, chop the mint and put everything in a jug. Now the whole thing can be poured with water and flavored with lemon juice and sweetener. You can also use lemon balm or basil. Other combinations are also possible.

Delicious shake with matcha

135.1 kcal | Protein: 15.7 grams | Fat: 5.1 grams | Carbohydrates: 6.6 grams

Preparation time: 4 minutes **Ingredients for one serving:** 150 grams of yoghurt | 50 grams of cottage cheese | 1 level teaspoon matcha powder | 1 splash of lime juice | 1 teaspoon natural whey powder | Sweetener or stevia as required **Preparation:** Put all the ingredients in the blender and process the whole thing at the highest level into a creamy shake. Now sweeten as you like.

Hot or cold chai latte

108.8 kcal | Protein: 11.8 grams | Fat: 6 grams | Carbohydrates: 1.9 grams

Preparation time: 6 minutes **Ingredients for one serving:** 150 ml Chai tea (Indian spicy tea) | 1 tbsp whey powder vanilla flavor | 50 grams of cottage cheese | 1 pinch of cinnamon | 1 pinch of clove powder | Sweetener or stevia as required. **Preparation:** Process all ingredients in a blender into a creamy shake. If you like the chai latte hot, use hot tea. For the cold version, use cold tea and also add ice cubes.

Fresh low carb berry shake

29.7 kcal | Protein: 1.1 grams | Fat: 0.5 grams | Carbohydrates: 5.2 grams **Preparation time:** 5 minutes **Ingredients for one serving:** 20 grams of blackberries | 30 grams of raspberries | 30 grams of strawberries | 3 mint leaves | 150 ml apple tea cold | 1 pinch of vanilla pulp | Sweetener or stevia as required **Preparation:** Put all the ingredients in a blender or smoothie maker and process everything into a creamy drink.

Low carb iced cocoa prepared with almond milk

67.7 kcal | Protein: 4.7 grams | Fat: 2.5 grams | Carbohydrates: 6.6 grams

Preparation time: 5 minutes

Ingredients for one serving: 200 ml almond milk | 2 tbsp whey powder with chocolate flavor | 1/2 teaspoon cocoa | 4 ice cubes

Preparation:
Put all the ingredients in a blender and work everything into a creamy mass. In no time you will have a delicious iced chocolate.

SHAKES, SMOOTHIES AND SNACKS FOR IN BETWEEN

Shakes are suitable as breakfast or as a general meal replacement. They are also quick to prepare and easy to transport if you want to take them to work. However, the amount of calories must also be taken into account here, as protein shakes can be very rich in certain circumstances.

Banana protein shake

234 kcal | 14.3 grams of protein | 0.9 grams of fat | 30.6 grams of carbohydrates **Ingredients:** 1 banana, 200 ml of milk, 100 grams of cream cheese, some sweetener, pulp of a vanilla pod **Preparation:** Put the banana, milk, cream cheese, sweetener and vanilla pod in a blender and mix everything together. The shake tastes best ice-cold. However, if you don't have time to let it cool in the refrigerator, just add a handful of ice cubes to the blender.

Exotic mango shake (Indian style)

223.5 kcal | 2.6 grams of protein | 15.1 grams of fat | 13.6 grams of carbohydrates **Ingredients:** 200 ml coconut milk, 1 mango, a piece of ginger, 1/2 pinch of cinnamon, 1/2 pinch of clove powder, juice of an organic lime, 1/2 pinch of turmeric **Preparation:** Put the ingredients together in the blender, puree and enjoy.

Fancy matcha shake with cream cheese

115.3 kcal | 13.4 grams of protein | 4.6 grams of fat | 2.4 grams of carbohydrates **Ingredients:** 1 teaspoon of matcha powder, 50 grams of cream cheese, 250 ml of soy milk, sweetener or xylitol for sweetening, juice of an organic lime **Preparation:** Matcha comes from Asia and is a green tea mixture that, like coffee, promotes energy. For healthy enjoyment, simply mix all the ingredients together and add ice cubes if necessary.

For all chocolate lovers

289 kcal | 5.8 grams of protein | 14.8 grams of fat | 27.3 grams of carbohydrates **Ingredients:** 50 grams of xylitol chocolate, 250 ml of low-fat milk, 1/2 pinch of cinnamon, pulp of a vanilla pod or a few drops of vanilla flavor **Preparation:** Liquefy the chocolate in a water bath and add the remaining ingredients to the mixer.

Warm and cold a pleasure.

A wonderful strawberry shake

164.7 kcal | 5 grams of protein | 0.6 grams of fat | 28 grams of carbohydrates **Ingredients:** 200 grams of strawberries, 1 chilli pepper, 200 ml of low-fat milk, 1 pinch of Himalayan salt, 1 teaspoon of xylitol or sweetener, juice of a lime **Preparation:** Simply mix all the ingredients well in the blender. The spiciness has a particularly stimulating effect on the metabolism and is wonderfully filling.

Nutty vanilla shake

189.4 kcal | 18.3 grams of protein | 10 grams of fat | 7.6 grams of carbohydrates

Ingredients: 250 ml of almond milk, pulp of a vanilla pod, 20 grams of whey protein powder, 1 teaspoon of hazelnut paste, xucker or sweetener

Preparation:
Again mix all ingredients together well. Of course we use a mixer

again for this. If you want, you can use a dollop of cream as a topping. Every now and then something is allowed to be sinned, this gives the shake a nice creamy note.

Green energy: avocado and mint shake

404 kcal | 25.4 grams of protein | 28.6 grams of fat | 12.1 grams of carbohydrates **Ingredients:** 1/4 avocado, 30 grams of whey powder, 10 grams of fresh mint, 200 ml almond milk, 50 ml cream, Xucker or sweetener as needed **Preparation:** All ingredients in the blender and make do by hook good. Full power thanks to this shake. The ingredients give you a real boost of energy, at the same time it is a successful breakfast substitute or good for in between meals.

Mixed Greek yogurt

234.5 kcal | 20.2 grams of protein | 0.5 grams of fat | 31.2 grams of carbohydrates **Ingredients:** 1/2 mango, 2 peaches, 150 grams of frozen raspberries, 200 grams of Greek yoghurt **Preparation:** Put the frozen berries in the blender with the other ingredients. Alternatively, you can of course also use any other berry fruit. So you can enjoy various combinations of berry shakes.

To enjoy: rice milk shake

313.8 kcal | 5.9 grams of protein | 20.6 grams of fat | 24.9 grams of carbohydrates

Ingredients: 250 ml of rice milk, 100 grams of pineapple, pulp of a vanilla pod, 30 grams of desiccated coconut

Preparation: Put all ingredients back in the blender. If necessary, the whole thing can be sweetened with a little xylitol sugar, birch sugar or sweetener.

Full energy against excess kilos

30 kcal | 0.6 grams of protein | 0 grams of fat | 4.9 grams of carbohydrates **Ingredients:** 1/2 cucumber, 1 bunch of coriander, 1 chilli pepper, 2 organic limes without seeds, sweetener as desired and water to fill up **Preparation:** Put the ingredients in the blender together with the previously peeled organic lime. At first the taste may take some getting used to, admittedly, but this shake is a real calorie burner.

The "green one"

245.2 kcal | 3.7 grams of protein | 15.2 grams of fat | 21.5 grams of carbohydrates

Ingredients: 1/4 cucumber, 1/4 avocado, 50 grams of spinach leaves, 10 grams of fresh coriander, 200 ml of coconut water (not coconut milk)

Preparation: Mix all ingredients together well and then simply enjoy. If you prefer it a little creamier, you can also use coconut milk instead of coconut water. But that's 200 calories more. So only as an exception!

Hot, hotter, chilli!

63.6 kcal | 1.8 grams of protein | 0 grams of fat | 12.9 grams of carbohydrates **Ingredients:** 2 tomatoes, 1/2 red bell pepper, 1/4 cucumber, 2 chili peppers, 1 pinch of Himalayan salt, 50 grams of mango, juice of an organic lime. Pour the finished drink with water or mineral water as desired. **Preparation:** Put everything back in the mixer and mix well. The hotter the shake, the better it gets the metabolism going. But beware! Do not exaggerate...

Passion fruit and orange shake

114 kcal | 3.5 grams of protein | 0.5 grams of fat | 23 grams of carbohydrates **Ingredients:** 100 grams of passion fruit pulp, fresh or frozen, depending on your taste with or without seeds, 2 organic oranges, 250 ml green tea, sweetener as desired, ice cubes **Preparation:** Before putting the oranges in the blender, cut them into smaller ones Cut slices. This combination of flavors is a real experience for all those who like it fruity.

Banana and cherry duo

183.5 kcal | 2.5 grams of protein | 0.4 grams of fat | 40 grams of carbohydrates **Ingredients:** 1 banana, 150 grams of cherries, water and sweetener as desired. **Preparation:** The cherries and bananas should be frozen if possible. Then add 100 ml of water to each of the fruits and pour it into the shaker. The classic variation tastes best.

Healthy Cuba Libre (Alcohol Free)

Preparation:

Freeze Cola ligth or Zero in small molds. Peel the pitted limes and put them in the freezer as well. Wait about 2 hours and then put it in the blender. With this combination you will also go down well at every party if you are doing low carb.

Special: The low carb power protein

149.8 kcal | 14.2 grams of protein | 4 grams of fat | 12.9 grams of carbohydrates **Ingredients:** 200 grams of skimmed yoghurt, 1 egg white, 2 tablespoons of quark, juice of an organic lime sweetener as desired **Preparation:** Beat the egg white until stiff, stir the remaining ingredients until smooth and then carefully mix into the egg white. Now put the power egg white in the cold and spoon it before you go to sleep. Our power protein prevents food cravings at night. As soon as you feel cravings again, take this secret weapon with you. You will see it works ??